FRANCESCO FEDERICO MANCINI
GIOVANNA CASAGRANDE

PERUGIA

HISTORICAL AND ARTISTIC GUIDE

D1610967

Published by
ITALCARDS
bologna Italy

Holder of sole rights of sale:
Ditta W. PELLEGRINI
Via Cialdini 16 - Perugia - Tel. 075-73253

The editing of the text was carried
out in constant collaboration
with the authors.
In particular, however,
Francesco Federico Mancini
edited the historic-artistic part while
Giovanna Casagrande
dealt with the more specifically
historic part.

Fotometalgrafica Emiliana
particularly wishes to tank
the Tourist Office of Perugia
for their technical colloboration
and for their advice
in preparing this guide.

Impagination:
Federico Frassinetti

Photographs:
Photographic Archives
Perugia Tourist Office
(photos Paoletti, Sacco, Tirilli)

Photographic Archives
of the Art History School of
the University of Perugia
(photos Giorgetti - Rome)

Foto Misano di A. Ascani
Foto A. Pesante - Perugia

Photographic reproductions:
F.lli Colombo Fotolito - Milan

PRESENTATION

*The historic-artistic interest of Perugia, the
increase and the notable results which the studies on Umbrian art have recorded over the
last decade and finally the request of a well-
informed and ever increasing body of tourists,
have made it necessary to provide the city with
a guide which, while still being easy to consult
and with a practical structure for itineraries,
also answers the new cultural requirements in
full. Such were the reasons which motivated
and which are perfectly satisfied by this new
guide to Perugia, printed by Fotometalgrafica
and prepared by two young but expert scholars: Francesco Federico Mancini, lecturer in
the School of Art History of the Faculty of
Arts of Perugia and Giovanna Casagrande of
the School of History of the same Faculty.*

*The collaboration between an historian and
an art historian, which is the basis of this
work, combines the modern outlook of the undertaking together with that inter-disciplinary
practice which has now become the basis for
all serious research.*

*Thus, while the ever-present historical sup-
port frames the artistic aspects in a wider con-
text of human events, the list of monuments
studied is much richer than the viewpoint of
traditional culture presented it in the guides
available to date. In fact, apart from the interest in the great artistic town heritage of the
Middle Ages and of the early Renaissance, all
the other evidence can be finally found in these
pages which the mannerism of the second half
of the 16th century, the baroque and neo-
classic periods and the 19th century, left in the
city. And it is in these sectors where the results
of the most recent studies are gathered, disco-
vering the continuity of an artistic tapestry
which has never faded and which is rich in
works of art; from the fascinating frescoes of
the Perugian baroque mannerism to the ora-
tors of the 16 and 1700s, from the masterpieces
of the great Baroque masters such as Algardi
and Lanfranco to the fantasy of Montanini's
landscapes to the documents of academic culture such as the stupendous collection of plaster casts of the Academy. An extremely rich
illustrative heritage, from which emerges immediately a new image of this city which see-
med to be permanently identified with the Pisano and Agostino di Duccio marbles and with
Perugino's paintings and frescoes, an analyti-
cal index which does not leave out the numerous formerly forgotten small monuments and
finally a precious bibliographic inventory including more than 400 items divided into sectors, complete this guide which, it is easy to fo-
resee, will be of use not only to tourists but also to students of Perugian art.*

ALESSANDRO MARABOTTINI

Historical background

Perugia is a typical example of an Etruscan and Roman city. For centuries its urban area was confined within the powerful city walls of the *urbs vetus*. After the year 1000, it began to expand progressively until the thirteenth century and first half of the fourteenth century, when the outlying hamlets became an integrated part of the city surrounded by a new city wall.

Like all Etruscan strongholds, Perugia is located on a hill (493 metres above sea level). It is not known for sure when the original urban nucleus was formed (6th century B.C.?). Traditionally, Perugia was the seat of one of the 12 «lucomonie», a clear indication of its importance as an Etruscan town. The ancient walls (6th-2nd century B.C.) and its various hypogeums are also evidence of this fact.

After the year 1200, Perugia became part of the Roman domain. Its fidelity to Rome continued even after the defeat of the Romans at Trasimeno (217 B.C.) during the Punic War. After 90 B.C., Perugia was conceded Roman city status. There is no documentation of the important events in which the town participated up to the *Bellum Perusinum* when it became the centre of the quarrel between Octavian and Lucian Antony, brothers of Mark Antony. Besieged, the city surrendered in 40 B.C., was burnt and partially destroyed. Following this event, Octavian Augustus had the town rebuilt and it became part of the 7th Administrative Region (*Augusta Perusia*). Shortly after the middle of the 3rd century A.D., the Perugian Emperor, Vibio Treboniano Gallo awarded the city the title of «ius coloniae» (*Colonia Vibia*).

The exact period in which Christianity was spread to Perugia is unknown although, presumably, this occurred from the very first centuries onwards; by the mid-5th century, the Perugian Diocese had already been formed. In the political void of this period, the Bishop represented the only form of religious and civil authority; indicative of this fact is the episode involving Bishop Herculanus who, as leader of the Perugian resistance during the siege by the Gothic King Totila, was martyred by him after the defeat of the city. With the end of the Greek/Gothic war (535-553), Perugia returned into Byzantine hands, becoming part of the strip of territorial land connecting Rome to Ravenna (the Byzantine Corridor), and a seat of the Exarchate.

The centuries leading up to the year 1000 are in the darkest in the history of Perugia. Althouth threatened and sometimes occupied, Perugia never fell to the political reign of the Longobardi who had conquered the nearby Dukedom of Spoleto; if anything, it was one of the cities under papal government. The advent of the year 1000 brought with it signs of social and political activity: as well as the Bishop, there were judges and «boni homines».

We do not know about the early phases of the Perugian commune which, by 1139,

Perugia, seen from St. Peter's Gate

had already been in existence for some-time. In fact, during this same year, the inhabitants of the Polvese Isle and Lake Trasimeno made an act of submission to the *civitas Perusina*, represented on the occasion by ten Consuls, the largest number possessed by any town at this time. During the second half of the 7th century, Perugia extended its dominion in various directions to include Gubbio, Città di Castello, Città della Pieve and towards the Trasimeno and Chiano Vallies. In 1184, it conquered Castiglione del Lago and began its conquest of the particularly fertile Chiugi area. In 1186, Emperor Henry VI conceded to Perugia the government of its «contado» by way of recognition of an already irrefutable fact. In 1198, Pope Innocence III took the city under his protection.

Being free of the Imperial Yoke, protected and favoured by the papal authorities and consistently Guelf (Ghibelline unrest was quashed as in the era of Corradino di Svevia), in the 13th century, Perugia was able to assert itself as a strong and powerful commune. It continued its policy of expansion conquering Assisi, Nocera, Gualdo, Montone and Cagli and was engaged in bitter fighting with Foligno. It had a city population of about 28,000 with 45,000 in the «contado»; alongside the original feudal nobility, a new bourgeoisie of merchants, artisans and lawyers etc. developed: in 1286, the varions artisan guilds numbered 41; the Mint and the University were instituted; public works, such as the aqueduct and the Great Fountain, were carried out; statutary laws were elaborated — the oldest statute of the city is dated 1279. Charitable institutions established themselves in the expanding quarters of the city in which several Popes chose to reside; indeed, four Conclaves were held there (1216, 1265, 1285 and 1294); many fairs were held such as the All Saints' Fair documented as early as 1260; the Discipline movement fostered by Raniero Fasani spread from Perugia (1250) throughout Europe; the city possessed two guest magistrates: the Captain of the People and the Podestà. The city was divided into five *rioni* (quarters) according to it porte (city gates) (porta Sole, porta St. Pietro, porta Eburnea, porta St. Susanna, porta St. Angelo).

During the first half of the 12th century, the first decades of Pope Avignone's reign, Perugia became even more independent in the assertion of its predominance. From 1303, the city's government was in the hands of Priors elected by the

4

Guilds (numbering 10-2 for each porta): this was the heyday of the guild-based commune. The important vulgate constitution dated 1342.

The black plague of 1348 also claimed victims from Perugia. The city gave further proof of its strength when, in 1358, it fought against the Cortonese and Sienese peoples (the Victory of Torrita).

The internal quarrels between the «nobles» (beccherini) and the «popular class» (raspanti), the attempts of the Papacy from 1350 onwards to subject the cities of Umbria to its authority, the war with Pope Urban V, ending with the Peace Treaty of Bologna (1370) in which Perugia recognised its subordinacy to the Roman Church and the Pope, all signalled the beginning of the city's political decline.

From 1370 onwards, Perugia was placed under the control of papal delegates; one of these, Gerard du Puy, Abbot of Monmaggiore, in order to keep a tighter hold on the city, had a fortress built at the porta Sole, linking it with the other one in the quarter of St. Antony. In 1375, the Perugians revolted and forced the detested Abbot out of the city, destroying both fortresses. Notwithstanding the banishment of the papal delegate, Perugia continued to be divided by internal party quarrels throughout the last 20 years of the 14th century.

At the beginning of the 15th century, the popular party, who had been led by Biordo Michelotti, killed in 1398, was in power, threatened, however, by the nobles. The popular government had to seek external support - first, from Gian Galeazzo Visconti, Governor of Milan (1400), then from the Church (1403) and then from Ladislao di Durazzo (1408). The power of the popular party declined between 1416 and 1424 and the governorship of Perugia was taken over by the famous mercenary captain, Braccio Fortebracci da Montone. After this, the city turned once more to the Church. The

The Etruscan walls of the Cupa

The Mediaeval wall of Porta St. Antony

governorship of Nicolò Piccinino, another mercenary, proved to be little more than a shadow of the preceding one.

The political government of «democratic» Perugia became more and more oligarchical and feudal, progressively losing alla forms of political initiative.

Among the families of the «old» and «new» nobility who were destined to from the oligarchical clique which would pull the strings of government in Perugia and the surroundig area are the folloing names: Baglioni, Oddi, Montesperelli, Montemelini, Arcipreti, Cavaceppi and Alfani — all descended from Bartolo da Sassoferrato — Paolucci, Tassi, Randoli, Corgna, dell'Antognolla, della Penna, Cinaglia, Graziani, Bontempi, Ranieri, Sciri, Mansueti, Armanni, Coromani and Signorelli etc. An important member of the Baglioni family was Braccio (died 1479), the so-called Lorenzo the Magnificent of Perugia; he too was a mercenary by profession. In 1471, he took part in the institution of Perugia's first printing guild.

During the 15th century, the economic strength of the «bourgeois» nobility and the «feudalised bourgeoisie» was based on territorial possession as well as on the predominance of certain key sectors of commerce and production.

15th-century Perugia — disturbed by feuds between the families of the oligarchy (Baglioni, Oddi, etc.) and by continual party struggles — was living a double reality: on the one hand, corruption and moral decadence and, on the other, religious fervour and moralistic ideals spread by the great Franciscan preachers such as Bernardino da Siena and Bernardino da Feltre. In 1462, Perugia's first pawnbrokers institution was established.

After betrayals and blood-shed in which members of the Baglioni family turned against and killed eachother (the «Bloody Wedding» of 1500), Giampaolo I and Malatesta IV, both of the said fami-

6

ly and both mercenaries, «governed» Perugia during the first decade of the 16th century. One was beheaded by Pope Leone X in 1520. The other defended the Florentine Republic against Pope Clement VII's army in 1529 (not without accusations of betrayal). However, not even the Baglionis succeded in establishing a governorship similar to that of the Medici family in Florence mainly because of the city's close proximity to Rome; indeed, the city was heading towards the total and definitive loss of its independence.

When the Perugians rebelled, refusing to pay a new salt tax, Pope Paul III took drastic action. He dismissed the priors and entrusted the task of government to the papal delegate, building in a very short time (1540-1543) the famous Rocca Paolina in order to keep the city under control once and for al. Although Julius III restored Perugia's magistrates (priors etc.) in 1553, by this time the Church's authority was absolute.

During the 17th century and most of the 18th century, Perugia was not the scene of great events. A certain «disorder» brought about the Castro War (1641-1644) between Urban VIII and his feudal lord, Odoardo Farnese.

Throughout the 17th century, the city's economic wealth was based on the agricultural nobility who had undertaken public offices. Associations, such as the Merchant's Guild and the Exchange, had undergone a complete transformation: from free associations for members of the relative trades, they had become exclusive institutions for the nobility.

The long period of «order» was shattered by the French invasion in which Perugia became part of the Trasimeno department with a consequent revival of the middle classes.

In 1831, after the Restoration, Perugia also participated in the revolutionary underground movements agitating against the Papal State. Here, too, patriotic and risorgimental ideas circulated. Domenico Lupattelli of Perugia died in the expedition of the Bandiera Brothers (1844). In 1848, the city rebelled and sided with the Roman Republic. In 1859, Perugia again rose against the Papal government and, in 1860, it was annexed to the Italian State; from then on, it has participated in all the great historical events: the 1915-18 war, Fascism (it was not lacking in opposers) and the last war. Around the end of the 19th century and during the first decades of the 20th century, the agricultural bourgeoisie and entrepreneurs came into their own, gradually displacing the hegemonious aristocratic nobility.

With the «boom» of the 60's, Perugia took on a new physionomy, expanding and developing in an irrational way, forming new urban quarters. The two universities for foreigners and Italians have given the city a dynamic cultural rôle.

The area around Porta St. Angelo

The Main Square: the Great Fountain and the Priors' Palace

The Main Square
(Piazza 4 Novembre)

The commune's main square — *platea comunis* or *platea magna* — was the centre of civil and religious power. In this area, the most ancient public building on record was the Consul's Palace, later the Podestà's Palace, which was located in the area around the Maestà delle Volte Church. Several fires and the reconstruction works carried out during the second half of the 16th century left no trace of this palace. The arches visible on the façade of the existing Bishop's Palace are perhaps remnants of the building's recon-

struction carried out around 1422-1423. The building in question was linked to the St. Lawrence presbytery to the north and to the Bishop's Palace to the south; the latter is thought to have been placed further back than the existing one.

The Priors' Palace
(Palazzo dei Priori)

A new residential palace for the highest ranking political authority of the city-state was thought of as early as 1270; by 1298, an early nucleus of the palace is

thought to have already existed, comprising the work of two local master-builders: Giacomo di Servadio and Giovannello di Benvenuto. From 1300 onwards, the Commune succeeded in making the necessary expropriations for the definitive construction of the *palatium novum comunis Perusii*. Amongst the buildings demolished to make way for the enlarged palace was the parish Church of St. Severo di Piazza. The construction work went on until 1353. From 1429 to 1443, a further extension was carried out. The later structural additions on the South side date from the late 16th century (1576-1588).

The palace is built in local Travertine and white and red Bettona rock and presents a compact and wall-like solidity. It is, however, animated by expressive decorative motifs and by the asymmetrical arrangement of spaces as on the side facing the fountain: here, the main portal is off-centre with respect to the façade and the levels of the two ensembles left and right of the fan-shaped staircase are different from eachother. This does not mean that the palace is lacking in stylistic unity or architectural coherence. These are guaranteed by the closely-placed succession of elegant mullioned and lancet windows placed in a rectangular display (lower level) and surmounted by a triangular apex

The Priors' Palace

The Priors' Palace: detail of the façade and the tower

(upper level). The façade which looks onto the fountain has a wide, semi-circular stair-case, built in 1902, the old version (designed by Ambrogio Maitani) having been destroyed at the end of the 16th century. From the first landing on the right, a staircase leads to the Vaccari Sala, the ancient seat of the Communal Cadastre (the iron door bears the initials «A.G.» — *Armarium Generale* — and the inscription «*MCCCXXXVIIII Giulius Rufinelli me fecit*»). Above the great ogival door there are two travertine corbels which acted as supports for the splendid mediaeval bronzes (late 13th-century) of the Griffin, emblem of the city, and the Lion, which are now preserved in a hall within the Palace. The same door leads to the NOTARIES' ROOM, originally an assembly hall for the people of Perugia. This is a majestic rectangular hall whose vault is supported by eight powerful Romanic arches. The frescoes depicting legends, tales, maxims, biblical stories and the coat-of-arms of the various Captains of the People and Podestàs are of particular interest. They were probably painted during the last decade of the 13th century by local artists, although they were restored and completed by the Perugian, Matteo Tassi around 1860. Recently, the name of the Maestro del Farneto has been suggested as the painter of those stories involving a rather static composural style, a monumental deliniation of figure and a dramatic and clear form of expression with hints of the archiac (Gideon and the Angel, Moses and the Burning Bush, the Egyptians following the Jews etc.). The scenes of a more immediate and vibrant pictorial effect, involving an attentive rendering of perspective and a controlled and precise narrative eloquence (Moses and Aeron talking to the Pharaoh etc.), are attributed to the expressionist, Maestro di Santa Chiara (Palmerino di Guido).

Returning to the exterior, before proceeding along the side of the building, there is a 14th-century portico with irregular arches on Roman-style capitals, two of which were made by «Vester Lutii»; this indicates the former site of the

11

Church of St. Severo which was demolished at the beginning of the 13th century to make way for the extension of the palace. The façade overlooking the Corso follows a curved line — obviously to adapt the extension to fit in with the pre-existing houses further back. Besides a progression of mullioned and lancet windows which lighten the solid horizontal effect of the wall, there is an elaborate rounded doorway attributed to various artists from Perugia, Siena, Florence and the North of Italy. On each side of the door there are pillars supported by lions: the one on the right bears allergorical sculptures of Generosity, Fertility and Pride; the one on the left shows Avarice, Greed and Humility. The pillars are surmounted by two griffins subjugating calves, symbols of the Butcher Trade which provided the majority of the funds for the realization of the project. In the splay of the portal, placed within animalistic and plant-like decorative motifs, the are 58 allegorical motifs which are often difficult to interpret. Finally, there are three statues of St. Louis of Toulouse, St. Lawrence and St. Herculanus.

The Priors' Palace: the door facing onto Corso Vannucci.

Within the palace, on the third floor, there are the headquarters of the Communal Administration. Of note, is the fine Gothic structure of the atrium with cross-vaulting supported by powerful columns. This floor is host to murals by Giovanni Schepers and Dono Doni (Sala Rossa), Giovan Battista Lombardelli (Urban Office), Bernardino Pinturicchio (Sala Consiliare), and Paolo Brizi (the Mayor's Apartment). The decoration (much repainted) of the vault and walls of the Sala Gialla, formerly the Chapel of the Priors' Palace, are probably the work of Matteuccio Salvucci.

The National Gallery of Umbria

The Gallery is on the third floor. It is the most important collection of mediaeval and modern art in the whole region. Its origins are in the state confiscations of the first French Republic and the Napoleonic Empire in which many works of the city's churches, convents and monasteries were gathered together under one roof: the Monastery of Monte Morcino Nuovo, especially provided by the Napoleonic régime. This concession was confirmed by Pope Pius VII during the Restoration. In 1861, in accordance with the Pepoli decree, designed to suppress religious associations, numerous other works were added to the Gallery which, in 1863, was named after Pietro Vannucci, alias the 'Perugino'. In 1879, all the material was transferred to the top floor of the Priors' Palace. In 1907, on occasion of the famous exhibition of Umbrian Sacred Art, this rich and well documented collection, arranged by Francesco Moretti, was officially inaugurated. During the period 1952-55, further acquisitions and, above all, the prevalence of new ideas regarding exposition techniques, led to a new arrangement of the material by Gisberto Martelli and Francesco Santi. The recent acquisition of greater exhibition space, including the large Podiani Hall, formerly the «Augusta» Communal Library, has brought about a further extension of the Gallery which now includes work from the Italian Cinquecento to Settecento.

12

The Priors' Palace: the Notaries' Room.

A visit to the Gallery begins in the MAIN HALL (Sala Maggiore) which was originally used as a meeting place of the Communal General Council. It contains numerous 12th and 14th century frescoes, mainly from Perugian churches, monasteries and convents. They constitute an important representation of local art, particularly of the Trecento, demonstrating, not without original contributions, the great Sienese and Florentine tradition which reached its ultimate expression in the pictorial cycles in the Basilica of St. Francis of Assisi. Of major interest are the following works: a 12th-century fragment with figures (no. 9); a group of frescoes originating from San Francesco al Prato (nos. 995, 1000, 1001); numerous paintings from the now demolished church of St. Elizabeth (nos. 670-671, 698, 700, 710, 712, 717); a large paiting of Our Lady of Mercy dating 1376 (no. 53); a Giottesque Angel after the style of Allegretto Nuzi (no. 440); a precious wooden cross from the Roman epoch from the Church of St. Mary of Roncione near Deruta (no. 925); a Head of Christ in carved wood, from Montone; a fragment of a 13th-century painted cross (no. 20).

ROOM I is dedicated to Umbrian art of the second half of the 13th century. Among the most important works are the following: the large painted cross from the Church of St. Francis al Prato, (1275) (no. 26), probably by an Umbrian artist commonly known as the Maestro of St. Francis; several sections of an altarfrontal by the same artist (nos. 21, 22, 23, 24) to which the double-faced processional cross (no. 18) probably belongs; a Giottesque altar-frontal, thought to be the work of the so-called «Maestro del Farneto» (no. 77); an altar-frontal by Gian dell'Umbria in a refined Byzantine style, following the example of the Roman model (no. 937); a small tabernacle adorned with dramatic and popular decorative motifs (no. 877); a pentych (no. 32)

The «Maestro di St. Francesco»: Crucifixion
(13th century)

Duccio di Boninsegna: Madonna and Child
(14th century)

by Vigoroso da Siena (1280); a precious Madonna and Child by the Sienese artist, Duccio di Boninsegna (no. 29); two sculptured panels from the Great Fountain of Perugia showing Rome and the She-wolf suckling the twins, placed in the Gallery for preservation, by Giovanni Pisano and Nicola respectively.

SALA II is entirely dedicated to the sculptures of Arnolfo di Cambio, parts of the dismantled fountain «in pede platea» sculpted by this Tuscan artist in 1281 by order of the Perugian magistrates (nos. 895, 896, 894, 1069).

ROOM III is host to numerous works by the Sienese artist, Meo, active in Perugia between 1320 and 1330 circa as well as a large altar-piece from the Celestina Abbey, signed by Marino da Perugia, a follower of Giotto, though also influenced by the artistic schools of Siena and Rimini.

ROOM IV contains 14th-century works by Perugian artists revealing a refreshing, albeit popular, narrative style, as in the works of the Maestro of Paciano (nos. 61,

65, 76, 81), the Maestro of Subiaco (nos. 11, 25, 28, 33, 981) and the Maestro of the Maestà delle Volte (no. 69). However, there is no lack of high artistic quality as is demonstrated by the fine stained-glass window by Giovanni di Bonino of Assisi (no. 68).

The continuous contact between the Sienese and local artistic cultures persisted throughout the second half of the 14th century and into the first decades of the successive one as is shown in the altarpieces by Luca di Tommé (no. 947), Bartolo di Fredi (no. 88), Taddeo di Bartolo (nos. 62-67, 72), Domenico di Bartolo (no. 116), Lippi Vanni (no. 59), Nicolò di Buonaccorso (no. 70) and Jacopo di Mino del Pellicciano (no. 58) which entirely occupy ROOM V. In the centre, is placed the bronze ensemble of griffins and lions, one of the last additions to the Great Foun-

Arnolfo di Cambio: A Scribe (13th century) ▶

**Gentile da Fabriano: Madonna and Child
(15th century)**

tain, which was transferred to the Gallery as it was thought to originate from a later time. In the same room is a rare sculpture in polychromatic wood from the second half of the 14th century, taken from the Church of St. Augustine in Perugia.

ROOM VI is occupied by works of the late Gothic period. It contains a fresco by the Salimbeni brothers (no. 986); an altarpiece by Lello da Velletri from Church of St. Agatha in Perugia (no. 123); a Madonna and Child with Saints (no. 1004), by the Eugubine, Ottaviano Nelli taken from the Church of St. Augustine at Pietralunga (1403); a polyptych by Bicci di Lorenzo from the Monastery of St. Agnes in Perugia (no. 79). Of particular interest is a panel by Gentile da Fabriano, one of the artist's earlier works, executed after 1408 for the Monastery of St. Domenic, Perugia.

ROOM VII contains precious works from the Tuscan Renaissance: the polyptych by Beato Angelico, made for the Guidalotti Chapel in the Monastery fo St. Domenic in 1437 (nos. 91-108); the polyptych by Piero della Francesca from the Monastery

of St. Antony, Perugia, one of the later works of the Artist of Borgo San Sepolcro (nos. 111-114); the Madonna and Child with Saints by Benozzo Gozzoli, signed and dated 1456 (no. 124); the fresco by Domenico Veneziano, a much-damaged fragment of the imposing series of famous men, painted around 1438, originally placed in the Palazzo of Braccio Baglioni which was destroyed when the Rocca Paolina was built (no. 443); the splendid bronze bas-relief of the Flagellation by the Sienese artist, Francesco di Giorgio Martini, almost certainly made in Urbino between 1478 and 1481.

ROOMS VIII and IX contain copious works demonstrating the diverse pictorial and artistic characteristic of Perugian painting during the period, 1450-1475. Alongside works by Giovanni Boccati, a refined and lyrical artist from Lippi, by dell'Angelico and also Domenico Veneziano (nos. 150, 151, 147, 148, 149, 437), ROOM VIII presents works by Matteo da Gualdo (no. 778); by Niccolò di Liberatore of Foligna, inappropriately nicknamed the «Alunno» (pupil) (no. 169); by Giovan Francesco da Rimini (nos. 126, 128); by Francesco Gentile da Fabriano (no. 879). In *rooms IX-XI-XII*, abundant space is devoted to the major exponents of Perugian painting in the late 1400's. Benedetto Bonfigli, a discipline of the Sienese Giovanni Boccati, who was also influenced by the painting of Benozzo Gozzoli and dell'Angelico, is represented by numerous altar-pieces among which, there is a particularly interesting Adoration of the Magi (nos. 140, 141), taken from the Monastery of St. Domenic and a fine polyptych (nos. 142-146), painted between 1466 and 1468, in collaboration with Bartolomeo Caporali who is certainly responsible for the part depicting the Annunciation. Caporali, an artist who moved from the styles of Benozzo and Boccati to that of Bonfigli and Fiorenzo di Lorenzo, is amply represented in ROOM XI with panels and frescoes ranging from 1469 to 1487 (nos. 166-170, 125, 160-63, 153-54). Part of ROOM XI and the whole of ROOM XII contain works by Fiorenzo di Lorenzo who progressed from a formation based on the ideas of Benozzo Gozzoli and the «Alunno» to a more mature phase founded on the new Florentine experiences of Verrocchio and Pollaiolo, attaining a form of artistic compromise between the work of the Perugino and Pinturicchio. Of particular interest is his Adoration of the Shepherds (ROOM XII), originally located in the Choir of the Church of St. Mary of Monteluce, Perugia, in which we note — particularly in his descriptive method — a relationship with the miniature works of Girolamo da Cremona and Liberale da Verona (nos. 178-179). Some early works of Perugino and Pinturicchio are exhibited in ROOMS XII and XIII. Among the most important works, is the Adoration of the Magi (no. 180), attributed by Vasari to the Perugino but in which there is clear evidence to suggest the collaboration of Fiorenzo di Lorenzo; the eight panels depicting the Miracles of St. Bernardino (1473) attached to a banner by Benedetto Bonfigli, one of the most fascinating and problematic critical puzzles of Renaissance Umbrian art (nos. 223-230). According to the most recent studies, two panels are attributable to the young Perugino and two to Pinturicchio; the others, however, are more difficult to identify (Bartolomeo Caporali? Bernardino di Lorenzo? Maestro dell'Annunciazione Gardner? Pietro di Galeotto?).

Beato Angelico: Madonna and Child among the Angels (15th century)

Piero della Francesca: the Annunciation (15th century)

Fiorenzo di Lorenzo: the Adoration of the Shepherds (15th century)

Bartolomeo Caporali: the Angel of the Annunciation (15th century)

ROOM XIV is host to paintings derived from the fully mature phase of Perugino's career: the dead Christ (no. 248), the Madonna of the Battuti (downcast) (no. 270), both dated 1495 circa, and sections of the great altar-piece of St. Augustine's painted between 1507 and 1523 (nos. 238, 243-245, 257-271). The altar-piece from the Church of St. Mary dei Fossi (or of the angels) by Bernardino Pinturicchio, an extraordinary masterpiece of descriptive imagination and chromatic richness, belongs to the artist's maturity.

ROOMS XV, XVI, XVII, XVIII, XIX, XX are dedicated mainly to Umbrian artists active in the first half of the Cinquecento who developed and elaborated the artistic language of Perugino to the extent of combining it with the Mannerism of Raphael and Michael Angelo, thus creating a cultural bridge between the Classicism of the early Cinquecento and the mature experiences of the Mannerist school. Among those included are the following: Giannicola di Paolo (nos. 320-325), Gio-

Benedetto Bonfigli (?): the Assault of the Captain (15th century)

Pietro Perugino: Christ in the Tomb (16th century)

Pietro Perugino: the Nativity (16th century)

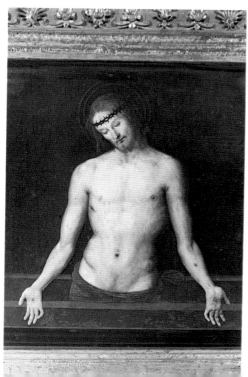

Bernardino Pinturicchio: Madonna and Child with St. John (16th century)

Giovan Battista Caporali: Madonna and Child (16th century)

van Battista Caporali (no. 27), Berto di Giovanni (nos. 294, 295, 303, 304, 307, 309, 318, 326), Domenico Alfani (nos. 288, 364, 354, 371-373, 341) and Pompeo Cocchi (nos. 275 and 669). Those more in keeping with the fifteenth century tradition are the following: Sinibaldo Ibi (nos. 352, 356, 357), Bernardino di Mariotti (nos. 155-157, 175, 176), Ludovico d'Angelo (nos. 232-234 and 265). These rooms also contain works by Piero di Cosimo (no. 983), Luca Signorelli and his pupils (no. 203), Dono Doni (no. 414), Orazio Alfani, son of Domenico (no. 368) and Vincenzo Danti. In ROOM XX, the frieze depicting the adventures of Braccio Fortebracci is attribuited to Papacello and Lattanzio Pagani.

The narrow 'Treasury' corridor (ROOM XXIII) exhibits gold-work from the 14th to 16th centuries. Among the most interesting works are the chalice and patena of Benedict XI and Sienese works dating from the early 14th century (nos. 743, 1013); the patena showing the Annuncia-

tion by Ugolino di Vieri (no. 1010); St. Juliana's relique case, also Sienese (no. 762). The chalice and patena signed by Catalucci da Todi is Umbrian and is dated around 1380 (no. 744). There are numerous precious works in ivory, one in particular showing a Romanic pastoral scene (late-12th century); there is also a late-13th-century statuette of the Madonna and Child, almost certainly French in origin (no. 869/363); and two containers which were carved in the Embriaghi workshop (no. 852 and 853). This small collection is completed by some wafer irons by Francesco di Valeriano, alias the 'Roscetto', a Perugian goldsmith of the late 15th century, and small bronze figures by Andrea Briosco, alias the 'Riccio' (puttino with shell), by Tiziano Aspetti (Venus and Love, Apollo and Venus) and by Vincenzo Danti (allegorical figures).

ROOM XXIV, the former Chapel of the Priors, is decorated with a frieze by Benedetto Bonfigli illustrating the lives of St. Herculanus and St. Ludovic (the work

Domenico Alfani: Madonna and Child between SS. George and Nicholas of Bari (16th century)

Agostino di Duccio: Madonna and Child
(15th century)

from the 17th and 18th centuries. The shorter wall is host to the great altar-piece by Cristoforo Gherardi and Lattanzio Pagani (no. 534) made in 1549 for the Church of St. Mary of the People. It combines the styles of the Aretine, Vasario (of whom, Gherardo, author of the upper panel, was a devoted follower and collaborator) with that of Raphael as interpreted by Giulio Romano and Polidoro da Caravaggio (Pagani, author of the lower section, was very clearly in contact with the Roman school as is evident from the quotation taken from Polidoro which is visible on the façade of the classic style building in the background). The considerable influence of the Flemish school in late-16th century Perugian art is evident in the large altarpiece by Arrigo Fiammingo, depicting the Adoration of the Shepherds (no. 477), whilst the popularity of the Baroccesque style, stimulated by the presence of this artist in Perugia (to paint a Deposition in the Cathedral) in 1569, in demonstrated in the works of Francesco Baldelli (no. 504), of Vincenzo Pellegrini, the so-called 'Pittor Bello' (no. 505), the San Diego altar-piece by Simone Ciburri (no. 1080) and several allegorical figures which

Andrea Sacchi: Presentation in the Temple
(17th century)

was partially completed in 1461 but, in 1477, Filippo Lippi added the finishing touches). Bonfigli also painted the first version of the Crucifix placed between St. Francis and St. Herculanus which was subsequently repainted by Arrigo Fiammingo in 1564. The floor made out of majolica from Deruta is modern (1954). It is, however, faithful to the original which was completed during the first half of the 16th century.

ROOM XXV preserves fragments of sculptures by Agostino di Duccio (1475 circa) which were taken from the Church of the Maestà delle Volte. The Madonna and Child, taken from a niche in the Church of St. Francis al Prato, and the two heads of angels from the Cathedral's courtyard, are by the same artists.

ROOM XXVI (or the Podiani Hall) marks the beginning of the modern of the Gallery which includes late-Mannerist works

Pietro da Cortona: the Nativity of the Virgin (17th century)

Orazio Gentileschi: St. Cecily and the Angel (17th century)

could be the work of either Benedetto Bandiera or Simone Ciburri (nos. 565-568).

The classical trends of the 17th century are represented by a Presentation in the Temple by Andrea Sacchi, taken from the Church of San Filippo Neri (no. 510), whilst, on the contrary, its 'baroque' tendencies come to light in the splendid canvas by Pietro da Cortona, a Nativity of Mary which also comes from the Church of San Filippo Neri (no. 535) and by a Mystical Wedding of St. Catherine, lent by the Academy of Fine Arts of Perugia. The influence of Caravaggio finds valid expression in the St. Cecilia and Angel by Orazio Gentileschi (no. 1083), and in the two canvases by the French artist, Valentin (nos. 1073 and 1074). 17th-century

◄ **Giovanni Antonio Scaramuccia: Madonna and Child between SS. Benedict and Catherine of Siena (17th century)**

Pietro Montanini: Landscape (17th century)

Umbrian art is documented by the presence of works by the following artists: Giovanni Scaramuccia (no. 476) and his son, Luigi (no. 503); Giovanni Domenico Cerrini (no. 880); G.B. Pacetti, the 'Sguazzino', and Pietro Montanini (no. 1088).

At the top of a spiral staircase in the interior of a tower along which can be seen a series of mediaeval prisons cells, there is a floor containing numerous 18th-century works. Of particular interest are the following: a canvas by Corrado Gianquinto (no. 379); a sketch by Francesco Trevisani (no. 614); three paintings by Sebastiano Conca (nos. 1070, 1071, 506); a large and dramatic painting by Ludovico Mazzanti (no. 545); an important altar-piece by Piere Subleyras (no. 543), taken from the Church of Monte Morcino Nuovo (the two small sketches on either side are also worthy of our attention); a work by Francesco Mancini dated 1732 (no. 541); a work by Giovanni Odazzi (no. 479); and, representing the artists of Perugia, two works by Giacinto Boccanera (nos. 484, 507); a painting by Anton Maria Fabrizi (no. 478) and two by Francesco Busti (nos. 483 and 542).

The final room is dedicated to Perugian topography, an exhibition of wood carvings and antique tableclothes.

Francesco Mancini: the Virgin, St. Joachime and St. Anne (18th century)

Pierre Subleyras: St. Ambrose absolves Teodosio of excommunication (18th century)

The Cathedral of St. Lawrence

(Duomo)

The Cathedral of Perugia originally stood in the area in which the Abbey of St. Peter is now located; it was then transferred to the area around St. Stephen's of Castellare, near the ancient city wall. Around the year 1000, the Cathedral was moved again to the city centre. In 1036, a refectory, other than the one reserved for the bishops, was certainly in existence. This proves that the Cathedral Church already had its own clerical community.

It was during the 16th century that the church took on its present-day appearance. Before that, it had been disposed and arranged in a different way. The original order for the construction of a cathedral church dates back to the year 1300; the works were entrusted to the supervision of Fra Bevignate, a Silvestrine monk. Notwithstanding this, its present form was acquired during the 15th century. As well as bearing the titular dedication to St. Lawrence, it was also given the title of St. Herculanus — the *defensor civitatis* bishop who was martyred by the Gothic King Totila according to a story by Gregorio Magno. During the «communal» epoch, Bishop Herculanus was the city's figure-head. Up to the 17th century, his remains were preserved in a specially-built chapel within the Cathedral walls; the walls of this chapel are still visible behind the statue of Julius III.

On the side facing the piazza, the arches of the **Loggia di Braccio** lean against the walls. The loggia dates from 1423 and is a monument of early-Renaissance architecture, attributed to Fioravante Fioravanti from Bologna. Below the Loggia, a section of Roman wall is visible. We can also see part of the base of the cathedral's former bell-tower as well as a copy of the Rock of Justice which is now preserved in the Priors' Palace. This is an object of considerable interest. Dating from 1234, it was constructed by the commune in order to mark the payment of all public debts and to establish the payment of taxes according to a census (*per libram*).

Giannicola di Paolo (?), Madonna delle Grazie

The church is composed of a nave and two aisles and is structurally based on the 'hallen' plan of the Church of St. Domenic in Perugia. Its external walls are incomplete in that they lack the marble covering which was part of the original plan except for the lower area of the side looking onto the Fountain, the covering of which was made from materials taken from the Cathedral of Arezzo in 1335.

On this side of the church, the bronze statue of Julius III, placed on a high pedestal, was made by the young Vincenzo Danti in 1555 to celebrate the Pope's restitution of the city's principal magistrates. The large, solid door is the work of L. Scalza (1568), based on drawings by Galeazzo Alessi. A niche above the tympanum of the door contains a wooden crucifix by Polidoro Ciburri, placed here by the people of Perugia in 1540 during the 'salt war', as an act of defiance against the Pope. The elegant Renaissance pulpit, right of the door, was erected during the first decade of the 15th century and it was from here that Bernardino of Siena preached in 1425 and 1427. Not far off, on a protruding column, there are two vertically placed niches; the higher one held a bronze statue by the Donatellian sculpture, Bellano da Padova. It represented Pope Paul II and was melted down by the French in 1798.

The principal façade, overlooking piazza Danti, has an impressive 18th-century doorway, built by Pietro Carattoli by order of Bishop Antonio Ansidei. The belltower was built between 1606 and 1612 by Valentino Martelli and was probably based on a design by Bino Sozi.

Inside the church, right of the door, the tomb of Bishop G.A. Baglioni backs onto the inner-façade wall. This is attributed to Urbano da Cortona. On the left, is the sepulchral monument of Bishop Marcantonio Oddi by Domenico Guidi, a pupil of Algardi. Above, within a frame of elaborate gold-plated stucco, is the great altarpiece by Giovanni Antonio Scaramuccia (1610-1611), originally destined for the Chapel of the Commune of Perugia in the church of St. Mary of the Angels. At the

Federico Barocci: Deposition (16th century)

beginning of the north aisle is the Chapel of the Holy Ring which contains the venerated relic of the Virgin's wedding ring, taken from Chiusi in 1473. The chapel was once decorated with frescoes by Pinturicchio. Now, a painting by G.B. Wicar is placed above the altar, substituting a painting of the same subject by Pietro Perugino, at present in the Museum of Caen. The altar is host to the precious reliquary of the Holy Ring by Bino di Pietro and Federico and Cesanno del Roscetto, a masterpiece of Italian Renaissance goldsmith work. Immediately following the side-door, we come across an altar of the Banner with a painting attributed to Berto di Giovanni (1526) and a lunette by Giannicola di Paolo. Further on, attached to the walls, are fragments of the Pietà altar, built by Agostino di Duccio around 1473 and demolished in 1625. The northern wing of the transept forms the Crucifix Chapel, the altar of which (the work of Pietro Carattoli), bears a carved wooden Crucifix dating from the 15th century. The chapel on the left-hand side of the apse contains a large canvas by Ippolito Borghesi (1624) depicting the Assumption of the Virgin Mary and frescoes by Francesco Appiani. The hectagonal apse, besides accomodating a splendid wooden choir by Giuliano da Maiano and Domenico del Tasso (1491), is host to two oil paintings by Baldassarre Orsini (1767) and two by Carlo Spiridione Mariotti (1768). The altar of the next chapel, named after St. Emidio, is decorated by a canvas by Francesco Appiani (1784). The south wing of the transept contains the Chapel of St. Stephen. This was once completely covered with frescoes by Giovanni Baglione (1609 circa). Two small side-doors lead into the Oratory of St. Onofrio, built in 1484, in order to accomodate the altar-piece by Luca Signorelli which is today preserved in the Cathedral Museum. The frescoes on the ceiling are by Domenico Bruschi (1877). Further along the south aisle is the Chapel of the Sacrament, built in 1576 and designed by G. Alessi. The altar-piece depicting the Pentecost is the work of Cesare Nebbia from Orvieto (16th century), whilst the lateral frescoes are signed by Marcello Leopardi from the Marches region (1795). The so-called Baptistry Chapel follows with frescoes by Domenico Bruschi (1876). The elegant Renaissance relief work on the far wall is the work of Pietro

di Paolo and Andrea da Como (1477). Opposite this chapel, on the third octagonal column of the aisle, is the venerated image of the Madonna of Grace, a work in the Perugian style, attribute to Giannicola di Paolo. At the end of the aisle is the splendid chapel of St. Bernardino of Siena standing behind a curious 15th-century wrought-iron grille. The most important painting in the entire church is located above the altar of this chapel: the Deposition from the Cross by Federico Barocchio. This was painted by order of the Merchants' Guild who owned the chapel during the period, 1567-1569. Outside the chapel, on the left, is a large painting of the Nativity of Our Lady, thought to be the work of Giulio Cesare Angeli (early 17th century).

Before continuing into the Sacristy, we may note the frescoes painted on the vaulting which constitutes a remarkable anthology of 18th-century Perugian painting; they include the work of Francesco Appiani, V. Monotti, V. Carattoli, C.S. Mariotti, M. Leopardi and D. Sergardi.

Passing through a small 15th-century doorway on the right-hand side of St. Emideo's Chapel (right of the apse), one enters the Sacristy, a large square-shaped room adorned with frescoes by Gian Antonio Pandolfi from Pesaro, dating from around 1578. The Martyrdom of St. Lawrence is depicted in the centre of the vault. From right to left, the corbels bear frescoes of the Arrest of St. Lawrence, St. Lawrence is tortured before martyrdom, St. Lawrence distributing the Church's possessions among the poor, the tyrant demands an explanation from St. Lawrence. Following the same order, the lunettes depict Noah's Ark (with a painting of the sybil Cumana on the corresponding vault section; Noah's drunkeness (the Prophet Elijah on the vault section), Samsom destroys the Temple (the Sybil Delphica on the vault section), the Indolence of Dagon (Daniel in the Lion's Den on the vault section), the Passage of the Ark of the Covenant over Jerico (Sybil Persica on the vault section) and the Conquest of Jerico (David with the head of Goliath on the vault section). The vault section above the large windows which are, unfortunately, virtually illegible, depict Jonah and the Sybil Frigia. The ovals depict the three theological virtues (Faith Hope and Charity) and Justice. The sidewall of the chapel bears monochromatic

Giovanni Baglione: The Stoning of St. Stephen (17th century)

images of the protective Saints Herculanus and Costanzo. The other wall bears paintings of the Four Doctors of the Church (Gregory, Ambrose, Augustine and Jerome). The bases of the thrones depict episodes from their lives in monochrome work.

The inlaid wardrobes are by the Eugubine artist, Mariotto di Paolo, alias the 'Terzuolo' (1497). The interiors of the doorways are decorated with an interesting series of saints (1601) painted by a Perrugian artists of the Mannerist school. On the far wall, there is a canvas attributed to Simeone Ciburri (18th century). To the right, is the Dean's Chapel which has a small painting of the Martyrdom of St. Lawrence above the altar, painted by Ferrau da Faenza, alias the 'Faenzone' (16th century). On the left, we find the meeting rooms of the clergy. The first of these has a vault decorated by a late-Mannerist artist who was probably commissioned by Bishop Fulvius della Corgna (second half of the 16th century). The Sacristy also leads into the old rooms in which the bi-

Berto di Giovanni: Banner (section) (16th century)

Gian Antonio Pandolfi: The Sacristy Vault (section) (16th century)

Anonymous (16th century): The Chapter House Vault

shops entertained their guests. One of these has a vault with frescoes by Marcello Leopardi depicting allegories of the Four Seasons (1795).

Leaving the Sacristy, we enter the 16th-century Cathedral Cloister at the centre of which stands a lovely 15th-century well which originally belonged to the Hospital of Mercy. Architectural fragments, reliefs, coat-of-arms, inscriptions and sepulchral slabs are attached to the cloister walls. Of particular artistic interest are a head attributed to Giovanni Pisano and a Renaissance bust of the Redeemer.

The **Museum** is host to works of art belonging to the Cathedral or to the Diocese of Perugia. It contains a large number of parchment manuscripts among which are fragments of a 6th-century Evangelistery; two Evangelisteries from the 8th and 9th centuries; an 11th-century Biblical Commentary; a Breviary from Maastricht (12th century); a 13th-century French missal; another small Missal dating from the second half of the 1200's originating from St. John of Acri with miniatures by an artist of the Venetian school; a group of 15th-century Antiphonaries, illustrated with miniature work which combines Giottesque elements, Martinian motifs and the French style of painting.

Among the paintings exhibited, besides the tryptych by Meo da Siena, there is a Madonna by Andrea Vanni and a tryptych by Agnolo Gaddi; there is also a splendid altar-piece by Luca Signorelli, painted for the Chapel of Bishop Vagnucci in 1484. Umbrian painting is represented by a Pietà by Bartolomeo Caporali (who also painted — in collaboration with his brother Giapeco — the miniatures of a late-15th century missal); a fresco of the Perugian school; an altar-piece by Pompeo Cocchi; a large canvas after the style of Girolamo Danti, commissioned by the Masons and Carpenters Guilds of Perugia during the second half of the 16th century.

In the room opposite, there are vestments, silver-work and a rare 13th-century faldstool.

On the left, we findt the entrance of the **Graduate Room** in which university degrees were conferred. Inside, we can see three frescoes: the one on the far wall depicts Pope John XXII between the Empe-

A missal with miniatures (13th century)

A miniatured Antiphonary (14th century)

**Luca Signorelli: Madonna and Child with
Saints (15th century)**

rors Charles IV and Sigismond I; to the
left, we see symbolic figures of canon and
civil law; on the right, there is an allegorical painting of Medicine next to St. Catherine of Alexandria, the patron-saint of
Study. This is probably the work of an artist from Assisi who was active during the
first decades of the 12th century. The
other two frescoes, as well as the illustra-
tions of the Judges Baldo and Bartolo

**Arnolfo di Cambio: Head of an Acolyte
(13th century)**

have been much re-painted, probably during the 19th century.

On the far left, one can look down onto
the first courtyard of the Presbytery with
three terraces dating back to the first half
of the 15th century. A total of three papal
conclaves took place in the Presbytery of
St. Lawrence (1216, 1265 and 1285).

The cloister also provides access to the
Domenican Library with its great wealth
of manuscripts and around 7,000-8,000
volumes.

**Meo di Siena: Madonna and Child with
Saints (14th century)**

The Great Fountain

The famous Great Fountain stands at the centre of the main square. It was built as a monument to mark the success of a public initiative, the completion of the aqueduct which carried water from Monte Pacciano directly into the main square. This project had been discussed as early as 1254. In 1277, the construction of the aqueduct, under the supervision of Fra Bevignate, was the Commune's prime consideration. The Fountain was erected in a relatively short time (1277-78) even though the water actually reached it a few years later. The architect and director of the works was Fra Bevignate; the hydraulic system was designed by Boninsegna da Venezia and the decorative sculptures were executed by Nicola and Giovanni Pisano. It is often difficult to distinguish between the work of these two individuals. Critics in general tend to attribute to Nicola those panels (most of the months, Adam and Eve, Romulus and Remus, Rea Silvia, Goliath and Samson and Aesope's Fables) and those images on the corners (Perugia, St. Peter, St. Paul and the Baptist) in which the influence of Classicism is more explicit with its controlled and compact solidity of forms. The work of Giovanni is characterised by a more accentuated linear tension and a stronger individuality of expression (Lake Trasimeno, the Chiusi area, Rome, the Roman Church, the two clerics, St. Bernard, Herman of Sassoferrato, Salome and Theology, among the corner statues, and the Eagles, Astronomy, Philosophy and Rhetoric, among the panels). In this period, Giovanni was on the threshold of his most original and mature period which was to culminate in his great decorative undertaking in the Cathedral of Siena. As for the group of bronze female figures which crowns the upper basin of the fountain, be they the work of Nicola or Giovanni, they represents a sublime expression of plastic sensibility and an extraordinarty composural harmony. The artistic perfection of the monument by no means detracts from its political and symbolic significance. Indeed, the Fountain, besides marking the urban renewal and extension of the piazza, was intended to

The Great Fountain (13th century)

35

The Great Fountain: Statues on the upper basin

The Great Fountain: the panels of the lower basin.

present an image of a city at the height of its political and cultural power, both internally and externally. It is a true reflection of the society which conceived and built it, bringing together themes from both civil and religious culture (the alliance of Guelph Perugia with Rome was of both religious and political significance) and uniting both sacred and profane elements demonstrating the possibility of ri-

conciliation between Man and Divinity, between religion and history. The fountain which we admire today was accurately restored in 1948-49.

The monument is composed of two polygon-shaped marble basins — one placed above the other.

The lower basin comprises twenty-five sections, each of which is divided into two panels. Beginning from the side facing the

Pietro Perugino: Ancient Personages and allegorical figures (16th century)

nise the hand of the young Raphael in certain figures eg. Strength and the face of Solomon.

The grotesque ceiling incorporates medallions in which pagan divinities in chariots pulled by various fantastic animals are depicted.

The room opposite was the seat of the Lawyers' Guild and contains benches which are the work of Giampietro Zuccari and his pupils (1615-1621).

Next to the Audience Room is the Chapel of St. John the Baptist who is painted by Giannicola di Paolo, a pupil of Perugino, who was also influenced by Andrea del Sarto and Sodoma (1513-1528).

Not far beyond the Exchange Building, on the left, one can turn into Via Mazzini, opened in 1547 and constructed by order of the Delegate Cardinal Tiberius Crispo. It was designed by Galeazzo Alessi who also designed the façade of the church of **St. Mary of the People** (no. 9) which is today used for secular functions. At the end of this street, we find ourselves in Piazza Matteotti.

Pietro Perugino: Mercury (16th century)

A detail of the Chapel of St. John the Baptist by Giannicola di Paolo (16th century)

During the Mediaeval era, this was the 'Piazza of the Wall', as it was built upon arches resting against the Etruscan Wall; it was also known as the Piazza Piccola in relation to the Piazza Grande of which we have already spoken. These two main piazzas were linked by a series of 'folds' which have now disappeared following modern reconstruction works. This piazza was host to the herb market and possessed several monuments which have either been destroyed or removed: in front of the Old University doorway, there stood the beginnings of a portico by Valentino Martelli (1591) which was never completed; its elegant central arch can today be seen infront of the Church of St. Francis al Prato. Above this arch, there stood a bronze statue of Pope Sextus V which was melted down by the French in 1798 in order to make coins; a 15th-century fountain was situated at the centre of the piazza.

◄ Pietro Perugino: Self Portrait (16th century)

The Old University Building (Palazzo dell'Università Vecchia)

The **Old University Building** marks the Western confines of the piazza. In 1266, Perugia either already had or was certainly in the process of planning a *Studium*; in 1308 — although university activity had in fact existed for sometime — Pope Clement granted Perugia the status of *Studium generale*. The building we see today dates from the second half of the 15th century. It is composed of a first floor of ogival gothic arches and a second floor with Renaissance-style cross windows. Sextus IV instituted the University's headquarters there in 1483 and they remained here until 1811. Today, the building accomodates the town's Magistrates Court. Long ago, the Hospital of St. Mary of Mercy had several workshops in the building; the architrave of no. 31 bears the hospital's coat-of-arms sustained by two griffins and dated 1472.

The Old University Building (15th century)

The Captain of the People's Palace

To the left, stands the **Captain of the People's Palace**, erected between 1470 and 1480 and designed by the Lombard masters, Gasperino di Antonio and Leone

Emblem of the Hospital of Mercy

di Matteo. Note the fact that the door is similar in type to the side-door of the Priors's Palace. It also has a fine loggia supported by consoles. The third floor was demolished after the earthquake of 1741. Today, this building also contains court offices.

Continuing along to no. 18-18a, two archways lead us to a renovated 14th-century loggia and the terrace which accomodates the town's indoor market (1932). From here, we can enjoy the splendid panorama of the Assisi Valley.

The Butchers' and Woolmakers' Guilds held there meetings in this area.

The Church of Jesus (Chiesa del Gesù)

The **Church of Jesus** is at the beginning of Via Alessi. It was built on the site of the former church of St. Andrew and of the St. Salvatore. Works on the church were begun in 1562. It was consecrated in 1571 and was extended around 1620 when

The Palace of the Captain of the People
(15th century)

the transept was added. After the suppression of the Jesuit Order in 1775, the church was entrusted to the Order of St. Barnabus.

The façade, originally completed as far as the cornice of the first floor, was finished in 1934 following a model found in a painting by Pietro Malambra which can be seen in the Umbrian National Gallery.

The interior has a nave and two aisles. The nave is composed of carved gold-plated lacunas by Girolamo Bruscatelli and Marco Pace from Perugia (16th century). On either side of the sumptuous main-altar, built in 1613 on African-black columns taken from the Church of Sant'Angelo, are two canvases by the Perugian artist, Stefano Amadei, depicting the Nativity and the Adoration of the Magi (17th century). The transept vault is completely covered with frescoes depicting the story of Joshua, painted by Andrea Carlone from Genoa (1656). The Sacristy, where the famous Madonna of the Cherry Tree was once preserved, today contains numerous pieces of valuable furniture in walnut, dating from the 18th century. The vault bears a fresco by Andrea Pozzi (18th century).

The church is surmounted by three oratories which, in their turn, are placed one above the order, forming a kind of tower corresponding to the apse. From the north aisle, a staircase leads to the Oratory of the Nobles (1596) which has frescoes by Girolamo Martelli and Cesare Sermei (17th century). Beneath this, according to a strict scale of social class, is the Oratory of the Artisan Congregation (1603) with frescoes by Anton Maria Fabrizi, G. Andrea Carlone and Cesare Sermei and two large lunettes by Paolo Gismondi (the Nativity of the Virgin) and Pietro Montanini (the Presentation in the Temple), both 18th-century Perugian artists. Again underlining the rigid adherence to class rules, the entrance to the third Oratory, that of the peasants (1603) is outside the church, in Via Augusta, a road which crosses Via Alessi. This is decorated with simple ornamental motifs by Pier Francesco Colombati (1746), a modest imitatore of Pietro Carattoli. On the left, at the far end of the Piazza, the suggestive Via Volte della Pace begins. This is composed of a long portico of pointed arches built during the 13th century along the path of the Etruscan wall. This road leads into Via Bontempi which we follow briefly, turning left into Via Raffaello, at the end of which we find ourselves in Piazza Raffaello.

The Church of St. Severo

The **Church of St. Severo** is situated in this piazza. Its present-day form originates from the 1750's. It was the seat of the Camaldolite Order from the beginning of the 11th century up to 1935, when it was taken over by the lay clergy. The interior follows the Neoclassical architectural model and has frescoes by Guglielmo Ascanio of whom a signed and dated sketch is preserved in the sacristy. The south arm of the transept, which forms a spacious chapel, contains a canvas by Francesco Appiani (1760), depicting Jesus Christ in glory placing a crown on the head of Blessed Michael the Hermit in company of SS. Scolastica and Antony of Padua. On the opposing altar, enclosed within an 18th-century tabernacle of gold-plated wood, is a figure of the Virgin of Sassoferrato (a copy of the original which is preserved in the parish centre). Above the main-altar is a large canvas by Stefano Amadei (1632 circa) dipicting the Virgin and Child among a company of Saints (Benedict, Romualdo, Severo, Andrew, Lucy and Catherine of Alexandria). The altar of the north arm has a painting of the Immaculate Conception by a disciple of Francesco Appiani (18th century). Beside the church is a 15th-century chapel which is a remnant of a renovation which took place in that period. The far wall bears the only certain work by Raphael to remain in Perugia. The upper section which is the one attributed to Raphael (1505-08), depicts the Trinity with SS. Marius, Placido and Benedict Abbot; on the left hand side are SS. Romualdo, Benedict the Martyr and Giovanni the monk. The lower section was painted by the Perugino in 1521; it shows SS. Scolastica, Jerome, John the Evangelist, Gregory Magno, Boniface and Martha. At the centre, within a niche, is a statue of the Madonna and Child in terracotta dating from the late 1400's. The fresco was restored in 1976.

From Piazza Raffaello, we proceed along Via dell'Aquila; turning left, we enter Piazza Biordo Michelotti; crossing this

Raffaello Sanzio - Pietro Perugino: the ▶ Trinity and Saints (16th century)

The Etruscan Well

piazza, after a brief descent, we come to Piazza Rossi Scotti. For a short period of time, this piazza was the site of an imposing fortress which was destroyed when the Abbot of Monmaggiore was banished from the city (1375-76); all that remains of the fortress are the huge arches which support a section of the wall. From this position, we can enjoy one of the many beautiful panoramas which Perugia has to offer. To the left, we can see the Porta Sant'Angelo quarter of the city (covering the area from the Foreign University to the Monastery of Monteripido); on the right, we see the bell-tower of Santa Maria Nuova, attributed to Galeazzo Alessi, and the Medioeval wall of the St. Antony quarter. Descending the steps of Via delle Prome (on the left), we arrive in Via Bartolo, directly in front of the Etruscan wall, with the famous Arch of Augustus a little further on.

On the corner of Via delle Prome stands the **Church of St. Angelo della Pace** (the Angel of Peace) the construction of which was ordered by the delegate Cardinal Tiberius Crispo. Traditionally, it has been attributed to Galeazzo Alessi but

modern scholars have suggested that it was designed by Raffaello da Montelupo. It was originally a loggia but was subsequently closed and transformed into an oratory. The adjacent building was the original seat of the Academy of Design.

The huge building on the corner between Piazza Rossi Scotti and Via delle Prome is the Palace of the Constable of the Cavalry, now the seat of the **Augusta Communal Library**, founded by Prospero Podiani in the 1580's. The Library possesses a conspicuous collection of volumes (early printed books, 16th-century works) and many precious manuscripts.

Following Via del Sole, we descend into Piazza Danti. Between this piazza and Piazza Piccino (no. 48), we come across the **Etruscan Well**. It is cylindrical in shape and the basin is composed of circular ashlar work. It is 35 metres deep with a maximum diameter of 5.60 metres. The exact date of the well is difficult to estimate: 400-200 B.C.? The large building on the shorter side of the Piazza is the **Turreno Theatre**, built in 1819 to a design by Alessandro Arienti; it was renovated in 1926 and 1953.

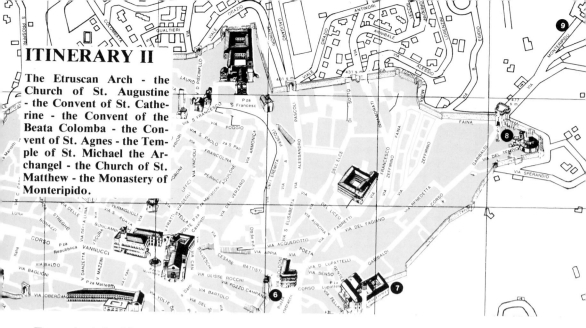

ITINERARY II

The Etruscan Arch - the Church of St. Augustine - the Convent of St. Catherine - the Convent of the Beata Colomba - the Convent of St. Agnes - the Temple of St. Michael the Archangel - the Church of St. Matthew - the Monastery of Monteripido.

From the left side of Piazza Danti, we turn into Via V. Rocchi, nick-named 'Via Vecchia' because of its antiquity. It was probably one of the five principal roads linking the 'borghi' (quarters) to the Piazza of the Commune. Its parallel, Via Bartolo, was opened in 1378. At the level of no. 34 is the former *Oradino College*, founded in 1582 by Polidoro Oradini to train young men for priesthood. It has an elegantly designed 16th-century doorway. At a certain point, we enter Piazza Ansidei with its attractive Palazzo Ansidei (18th century). At nos. 29-31 Via V. Rocchi, the façade of the ancient parish church of St. Donato can still be seen.

The Etruscan Arch

The Italian University for Foreigners:
main floor terrace

The Etruscan Arch
(Arco Etrusco)

Continuing to the end of Via F. Rocchi, we arrive at the **Etruscan Arch** (or **Arch of Augustus**), one of the seven or eight doorways of the *urbs vetus*, whose wall was 2.9 kilometres in length. Its imposing structure has always attracted great admiration. In a document dating 1036, it is referred to as the *Porta Pulchra* (= the Beautiful Door) but it had been thus defined since the late 7th century. Francesco Suriano, a Franciscan who lived in the 15th century, described the walls of the Egyptian pyramid as being «all covered with large life-like slabs of stone ... each fitting into the other *as in the city door of Via Vecchia in Perugia*, with marvellous artifice without mortar, each bound to the other...».

The Arch affords a frontal view of Piazza Fortebracci. It consists of two tra-

pezoidal towers with an ornamental façade in the centre. The barrel-vault is corniced by two concentric armillas and by a moulded cavetto with a frieze of triglyphs surmounting tapered Ionic columns and metopes with rounded shields; above this is an upper level consisting of an open arch between two Ionic columns; on top, is a Renaissance style loggia (16th century). On the two concentric borders of the lower arch are the words «*Augusta Perusia*» and, inscribed on the cornice below the frieze, «*Colonia Vibia*».

The fountain on the left was completed in 1621.

Piazza Fortebracci was built by order of the delegate Cardinal Marino Grimani in 1536. Apart from the Etruscan Arch, it is dominated by the imposing Palazzo Antinori, subsequently named after Gallenga Stuart, which is now the headquarters of the **Italian University for Foreigners** which opened in 1926.

It is an attractive 18th-century building in laterite stone, built by Pietro Carattoli to a design by the Roman architect, Francesco Branchi (1740-1758). The interior is decorated with frescoes attributed to Giuli and Carattoli; the third floor accomo-

The Italian University for Foreigners:
Palazzo Gallenga (18th. century)

dates a series of canvases commissioned by Girolamo Antinori in 1762. The building was enlarged, preserving, however, its original style, during the period 1935-37.

Between the Etruscan Arch and the University for Foreigners is the beginning of Via Cesare Battista, commonly called the 'Strada Nuova' (New Road) on account of its having been opened at the beginning of this century. This road links Piazza Fortebracci to Piazza Cavallotti. A considerable part of the road is bordered by the Etruscan wall and, from here, we can discern the subsequent course of the ancient wall towards the West (the Verzaro quarter).

Right of the Arch, is the **Church of St. Fortunato**, probably of paleo-Christian or high-Mediaeval origins. In 1163, it was listed among the dependencies of the Cathedral of Perugia. Without doubt, it was a parish church in 1285. In its present form, it has existed since 1633 when it was rebuilt by Silvestrine monks who had been transferred here definitively after the construction of the Rocca Paolina. The façade still reveals the structure of the Mediaeval church: it has a double-sloping roof and a trapezoidal bell-tower. It is an

aisless church and contains wooden gold-plated altars with French-style statues, some of which are by Leonardo Scaglia. The painting at the far end of the Chior, depicting the Madonna, St. Fortunato and St. Gregory, is the work of the Perugian artist, Scilla Pecennini. It was originally placed above the main-altar, now demolished, the decoration of which was executed by Bino Sozi in 1584.

If we continue along Corso Garibaldi (former Via della Lungara), we enter a typical 'popular' quarter, a lively and animated part of the city. During the Mediaeval age, it housed a mainly artisan population and it is a characteristic example of a new quarter which grew up outside the city walls.

The Church of St. Augustine

A short distance further ahead, we reach Piazza Domenico Lupatelli (a citizen of Perugia who died in the failed undertaking of the Bandiera brothers), which is dominated by the façade of the **church of St. Augustine**. The lower gothic section is overlaid with pink and white

The Church of St. Augustine: Interior (18th century)

Baccio d'Agnolo: Wooden Choir (16th century)

Francesco di Guido da Settignano: the Chapel of Our Lady of Grace (16th century)

Pellino di Vannuccio: Crucifixion with Sain (14th century)

slabs forming the chequered pattern so typical of Perugia (cf. the Church of St. Mary of Monteluce, the Church of St. Juliana etc.). It has twin-doors. Its laterite upper section is Mannerist in style and is attributed to Bino Sozi (16th century).

The Augustinians established themselves in the Sant'Angelo quarter of Perugia during the period 1256-60 and a Gothic church was built of which only a few chapels remain. The interior, as seen today, was rebuilt between the 18th and 19th centuries by Stefano Canzacchi di Amelia and is Neoclassical in style.

Some Gothic chapels are to be found in the northern part of the nave and at the beginning of the transept. The second chapel to the left of the nave contains a fresco depicting the Crucifixion by Pellino di Vannuccio (1377); the third chapel contains another fresco — a Madonna on the throne between SS. Joseph and Jerome — by an early 16th century artist. The fourth chapel has late 16th century decorations on its lunettes painted by Giovan Battista Lombardelli, an artist from the Marches region of Italy.

To the right of the nave, the first chapel is ornamented by Francesco di Guido di Viorio of Settignano in the Renaissance style (16th century). Here, we can admire a Madonna of Grace attributed to Giannicola di Paolo. In the second gothic chapel, there are two large canvases by Arrigo Fiammingo dated 1515 (Christ and St. Andrew) and 1560 (the Martyrdom of St. Catherine).

At the head of the transept, we find the remains of a chapel originating from the previous gothic structure. In the chapel on the right, there are frescoes attributed to Allegretto Nazi and Piero di Puccio of Orvieto (1398). In the south wing of the transept, is a Deposition from the Cross dating back to the second half of the 14th century. The wooden choir in the apse is the work of Braccio d'Agnolo, perhaps based on a drawing by the Perugino. The Perugino also painted the large altarpiece, today partially preserved in the Umbrian National Gallery.

Next to the Church is the **Oratory of the Augustinian Brotherhood**, built in 1317. We reach the interior via a passage containing frescoes by Francesco Appiani. Inside, we find one of the richest and most interesting ambients to be produced during the proto-Baroque period in Peru-

The Oratory of St. Augustine (17th century)

gia. The vault is made of carved, gold-plated wood and the stalls are the work of the French artists, Charles d'Amuelle and Monsù Filippe. The paintings on the wall depicting episodes from the lives of Jesus and SS. Phillip and James were realised between 1618 and 1630 and are the work of Giulio Cesare Angeli of Perugia with the exception of the last three on the right which are by Bernardino Gagliardo of Città di Castello (1656). The paintings on the vault are by Mattia Batini (1700). The altar, made by Marco Pace of Perugia to a design by Bino Sozi (1586), is host to a panel by Raffaellino del Colle (1563). The Sacristy contains perspective decorations by Pietro Carattoli (1762 circa) and paintings by Francesco Appiani. Above the altar is the processional banner by Giovanni Antonio Scaramuccia (1625) which depicts the Virgin and Child between SS. Augustine, Francis and Domenic. Beneath the Oratory, in rooms which, unfortunately, are not open to the public but which, because of their importance, should be pointed out, was the ancient seat of the hospice run by the monks. It is a huge ambient with cross-vaulting and 14th-century frescoes, among them, a Crucifixion attributed to the Maestro of Paciano; the far wall bears frescoes of the Crucifixion with the prostrate Virgin supported by St. John and Mary Magdalen, who is embracing the cross: this is a work of the Perugian school dating from the first half of the 16th century.

Ascending again, on the left, nos. 84-86, we can see some buildings bearing the coat-of-arms of the Merchants' Guild (a griffin clutching a bale): here, without doubt, up to the end of the 1200's the Guild had its hospice, next door to the **Church of St. Egide**. This church was restored in 1793 and contains frescoes by Anton Maria Garbi.

At no. 104, a small travertine archway marks the entrance of a charming hanging garden which looks out over the Verzano quarter of the town.

At no. 106, we can see the façade of the **former parish Church of St. Christopher**, already a parish centre in 1285 and today used as carpentary workshop. It has a canopied doorway.

On the right, nos. 133, 135 and 137, we find some characteristic houses with travertine walls dating from the early 15th century.

On the left, we take Via Benedetta which leads us to the former **Monastery of St. Benedict**. During the first half of the 15th century, this was the seat of the Augustinian hermits and was called the Monastery of St. Maria Novella; in 1640-41, Silvestrine monks from the monastery of St. Benedict moved there and, from them, came the title of St. Benedict Novello. The monastery was suppressed in 1820. It is now the headquarters of the University Opera House. The church contains a 15th-century majolica pavement; the second arch has a fresco depicting the Annunciation of the 16th-century Perugian school of painting. Above the main-altar is a canvas painted by a Perugian artist around the beginning of the 17th century; the Chapterhouse has a Nativity dating from the 16th century. The 18th-century bell-tower imitates the architectural style of Alessi.

The Convent of St. Catherine

Following Corso Garibaldi up to no. 179, we come to the Benedictine **Convent of St. Catherine**, built around 1547 to a design by Galeazzo Alessi. Its construction was sponsored by the Convent of St. Juliana whose sisters were its proprietors, having built it with the intention of moving there. It was probably the seat of the Convent of St. Clare which had been established in the 1380's. In 1647 it was taken over by the nuns of St. Catherine Vecchia who solemnly established themselves there in 1649. Inside the church, the vault bears frescoes depicting episodes from the life of St. Catherine of Alexandria by Mattia Batini and canvases by Benedetto Bandiera (St. Ursula and the Virgins; the Mystical Marriage of St. Catherine; the Crucifixion; the Descent of the Holy Spirit) and also by Batini (the Immaculate Conception).

The Convent of the Beata Colomba

At no. 191 is the **Convent of the Beata Colomba** (second order Dominican nuns), established, after the merger of this convent with that of St. Thomas (1940), together taking over the former Convent of Charity. Inside, there is a reconstruction of the Beata's cell (she was a mystic Dominican tertiary who died in Perugia in 1501) which contains relics of the same. Here, we find a suggestive pain-

The Church of St. Catherine: Interior (18th century)
The Convent of the Blessed Colomba: Giovanni Spagna (?) — Christ Carrying the Cross (15th century)

The Sperandio Gate (Porta Dello Sperandio)

The Convent of St. Agnes: Pietro Perugino
-The Crowned Madonna (16th century)

ting of Christ on the Cross attributed to Spagna (late 15th century). The church's left-hand altar has a canvas by L. Caselli which is an early 19th-century copy of the Disbelief of St. Thomas by Giannicola di Paolo, today preserved in the Umbrian National Gallery; above the grille behind the main altar, there is a painting by Francesco Appiani which was taken from the Monastery of St. Thomas. The vault was decorated by Nicola Giuli of Perugia (18th century).

Bordering the convent is a stretch of Via dello Spernadio which is interrupted by the Mediaeval **Porta Sperandio**. This low arch, in alternated travertine and sandstone is supported by two quoins which also form the piers. The arch bears an inscription which records the fact that in 1329 'porta ista restaurata fuit' (this door was restored). On either side we can admire the mediaeval walls of the city built in a combination of sandstone, calcareous and travertine rock. Proceeding forward from the Sperandio arch, we come to the former Convent of St. Sperandio,

supposedly established in 1262 by Abess Santuccia of Gubbio on land donated by Sister Sperandia Sperandei, also from Gubbio. Suppressed in 1799, it was used as a private villa. The external door still bears the inscription «Spera in Deo 1696». Nearby, a small convent was built by the Order of St. Speradio, possibly as early as the 13th century; of this convent, there remains part of the Cloister to be seen in no. 6, Via Sperandio (Casa Mori).

The Convent of St. Agnes

Following Corso Garibaldi, we turn left into Via S. Agnese which leads us to the abovementioned **monastery**; it was the seat of the Poor Clares during the year 1329-30; in the period 1428-30, it was passed into the hands of Franciscan Tertiary nuns who remained there up to 1911 when it was again taken over by the Poor Clares. The convent's church (17th century) contains canvases by Perugian artists of the period: Bassotti (The Flagellation of Christ) and Angeli (The Madonna and

Jesus Christ in Glory with St. Francis offering them roses, dated 1615; St. Agnes and other figures). In one of the arches of the Choir, on either side of a wooden crucifix, there are paintings of Our Lady and St. John the Evangelist; in the intrados, there are paintings of St. Sebastian, the Eternal Father and St. Rocco, attributed to Eusebio da S. Giorgio (1519). An internal chapel, which is nonetheless open to visitors, has a fresco by Perugino depicting Our Lady of Grace between St. Antony Abbot and St. Antony of Padua (1522).

In Corso Garibaldi, there existed two other female religious establishments: the Convent of St. Lucy of the Augustinian Sisters (today, the Antinori Conservatory) and the Convent of St. Antony of Padua of the Franciscan Tertiaries (today, a female hall of residence).

Opposite Via S. Agnese is the beginning of Via del Tempio. On the corner of this road and Corso Garibaldi there is a small chapel which is rarely open to visitors; it contains a venerated and miraculous image of the Virgin and a famous 14th-century fresco which has subsequently been repainted.

The Temple of St. Michael the Archangel

Via del Tempio takes us directly to the paleo-Christian **Church of St. Michael the Archangel**. Its origins go as far back as the 5th and 6th centuries; in 1036, it became a dependency of the Cathedral Charter. The central plan of the building is similar in type to the Church of St. Stephen Rotonda in Rome with four chapels fac-

The Temple of St. Michael the Archangel.

ing onto the ambulatory, each following the Greek Cross model. The central space is separated from the ambulatory by a circle of sixteen Roman Corinthian columns which support the tiburio, the materials used for these arches were obviously plundered from elsewhere due to the diversity of height and type of marble; the coussinets above the roman Corinthian style capitals give evidence of the Byzantine influence originating from Ravenna. The saddle-roof is supported by ribs resting on elegant corbels; these, together with the door-way, are of the Gothic period. Following the course of the ambulatory from the right of the entrance, we come across the following: a 14th-century fresco; the Baptistry with frescoes by a 15th-century Umbrian artist; the Madonna del Verde, a fresco originally situated in the cathedral which is a local work dating from the early 13th century, placed above a Roman tablet of the period of Marcus Aurelius. The altar is composed of a marble slab set above a drum.

On leaving the Temple, immediately on the right, we descend a small staircase which leads us to the **Tower of porta Sant'Angelo**. This is largest of the mediaeval city doors and was built in several different phases during the early 14th century; the interior reveals the wall of ashlar-work sandstone; the vault is made of bricks. In the piers, the slabs of travertine reveal the fluting necessary to accomodate a slide-door. From the exterior, it is easy to distinguish the three phases of construction and the various different materials employed in each: sandstone at the base, calcareous rock in the centre and brick in the upper regions.

The Church of St. Matthew

Beyond the tower, in Via Monteripido, the **Church of St. Matthew of the Armenians** is immediately on our left. In 1272, this site was donated to the monks of St. John the Baptist by the Canons of the Cathedral; the church was consecrated in 1273. Inside, the nave is subdivided into two parts. It is overhung by cross-vaulting resting on six huge columns which jut of the wall. The far wall has a large trilobated window and is adorned by important frescoes painted by a 13th-century Umbrian artist. They depict the Ascention of

The Temple of St. Michael the Archangel: Interior   **The keep of the St. Angelo Gate ▶**

N 21584

Perugia città museo

PERUGIA.

Pozzo Etrusco
Cappella di S. Severo

09 MAR. 1994
09 MAR. 1994

The Monastery of Monteripido

Christ, the Twelve Apostles, St. Matthew the Apostle and St. Francis of Assisi, the enthroned Madonna and Child with a Saint, probably St. Basil. The lateral walls bear votive frescoes dating from the 13th and 14th centuries. Of particular interest is a painting of the enthroned Madonna among the saints which is dated 1348 and was undoubtedly executed by a Perugian artist. Also of interest is a St. Leonard with a kneeling congregation.

The Monastery of Monteripido

Ascending a suggestive uphill-street, bordered on the right by the Stations of the Via Crucis (1633-1636), we arrive at the **Monastery of St. Francis of the Mount** (Monteripido). Among these hills dwelt the Blessed Egidio (+ 1262), one of the first disciples of St. Francis, near to the residence of the Noble Coppoli family and particularly under the 'protection' of Giacomo di Boncorte. In 1276, the latter donated the site on which he had lived including the house, oratory and other buildings, to the Minor friars of the Monastery of St. Francis al Prato in Perugia. From 1290 onwards, we have evidence of an active monastery community. In 1374, Monteripido was donated to Fra Paoluccio Trinci, a promoter of the Franciscan Observants' movement. From this time on, the history of the monastery is linked to that of the Observants who established a prestigious *Studium* for the monks of this Order. St. Bernardino of Siena stayed there several times and St. Giovanni of Capestrano was a novice there.

The church was reconstructed in a modern style by Tommaso Stamigni of Perugia in 1858. The interior, which still contains the chapel erected by Orazio di Bevignate Alessi in 1588 (with 20th-century frescoes), contains a fine wooden cross which is perhaps the work of Eusebio Bastoni (16th century). Backing onto the curve of the apse, is a Choir made in wal-

Anonymous 16th century artist: the Feeding of the Five Thousand

61

The Monastery Library (18th century)

nut by Girolamo di Ronaldo and Masco Pace between 1571 and 1581. This originally belonged to the Dominican monks. Behind the apse, there is a small chapel which is said to be the cell of the blessed Egidio, containing a much re-painted Crucifix by a 13th-century Umbrian artist. The first of the three cloisters has lunettes bearing much-damaged frescoes of the early 17th-century Assisi school. Those on the left are attributed to Anton Maria Fabrizi. The far wall of the refectory has frescoes by an anonimous Mannerist artist of the late 16th century, probably local in origin but including stylistic components characteristic of the Flemish school. On the left, there is a fresco of the Feeding of the Five Thousand; in the centre, the Crucifixion of St. Veronica and, on the right, the Refection of St. Clare.

The Monastery library with its well-preserved decorations and furniture (the library material is now to be found in the Augusta Communal Library), was built to a design by Pietro Carattoli between 1754 and 1790. Carattoli also designed the external achitecture and the walnut furniture.

From Monteripido, if we take the turning to the left, we arrive at the former **convent of St. Catherine**. It was abandoned by the nuns in 1643 after the Castro war when they moved to the new Convent (cf. Corso Garibaldi, no. 179) in 1949. All that remains of the old convent is the church which was restored at the beginning of the 17th century. In 1620, Cristoforo Roncelli, alias the «Pomarancio», was commissioned by Abess Cristina degli Oddi to paint the vault and medallions with the figures of St. Benedict, St. Scolastica, St. Catherine etc. The «domine Sancte Capterine» was spoken of as early as 1248.

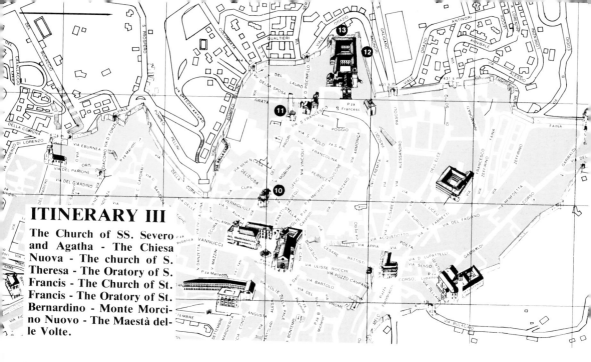

ITINERARY III

The Church of SS. Severo and Agatha - The Chiesa Nuova - The church of S. Theresa - The Oratory of S. Francis - The Church of St. Francis - The Oratory of St. Bernardino - Monte Morcino Nuovo - The Maestà delle Volte.

The first road to cross Corso Vannucci is Via dei Priori which begins under the great vault of the Priors' Palace. It is a characteristic road, typical of Perugia's historical centre, with openings into suggestive mediaeval side-road and numerous private and religious buildings.

After a brief stretch of this road, we turn into via della Gabbia (of the Cage) which leads back into the Main Piazza (Piazza IV Novembre). This road takes its name from the fact that it was here that condemned prisoners were exhibited to the blood hungry public. From here, we can see a tower which is completely incorporated into the Priors' Palace.

The Church of SS. Severo and Agatha

Continuing along Via dei Priori, we come across the **Church of SS. Severo and Agatha** on our left. It is probable that a pre-existing chapel to St. Agatha stood here; it is known for certain that the church we see today was built by the Commune at the beginning of the 14th century in order to compensate for the permission granted by the ecclesiastical authorities to demolish the church of St. Severo di Piazza in order to extend the Priors' Palace. As early as 1319, the «ecclesia nova Sancti Severi» was spoken of. Inside, there are frescoes dating from around the beginning of the 14th century:

on the lefthand wall, the Story of St. Severo after the style of Simone Martini and, on the far wall, the Crucifixion by an artist who was influenced by Pietro Lorenzetti (Maestro di Paciano?). There also numerous votive frescoes. Behind the altar is a polyptych showing Our Lady and Saints, a copy of the panel by Lello da Velletri, today preserved in the Umbrian National Gallery.

A short way further ahead, we can turn into Via Ritorta for a moment, in order to get an idea of the typical mediaeval streets in the area of Via dei Priori. At no. 22, we note a spiral staircase leading up to a house; at no. 14, there is an arched doorway decorated with gothic relief work depicting animals; at nos. 1 and 1a, we can see a characteristic mediaeval tower. On the right, there is the Church of the Maestà delle Volte (cf. further on).

At the beginning of Via Ritorta, no. 24 Via dei Priori, there is a fine doorway of a private house which was probably made by Valentino Martelli.

The Chiesa Nuova
(New Church)

Continuing along Via dei Priori, on our right, we come to the **New Church of St. Phillip Neri** or **of the Conception**. This

The Church of St. Philip Neri or The «New» Church: Façade (17th century)

church was constructed on the side of the early-Christian Baptistry of St. Giovanni Rotondo which, in 1618, had been given to the fathers of the Oratory Congregation whose arrival in Perugia (1614) had been solicited by Bishop Napoleon Conitoli. The first stone of this edifice which was to cancel all trace of the former one, was laid in 1626. The project was entrusted to the Roman architect, Paolo Maruscelli, whose design conformed to the dictates regarding architecture prescribed at the Council of Trent. The façade, similar to that of the Church of St. Susanna in Rome, was completed in 1665, whilst the longitudinal body and cross-wing of the church were built between 1627 and 1634. The dome was erected later in 1648.

It is an aisleless church, similar in style to the Church of St. Mary in Vallicella (or Chiesa Nuova) in Rome, and has a vaulted ceiling and side-chapels.

The vault was decorated in 1762 by Francesco Appiani with themes lifted from the Apocalypse of St. John. The chiaroscuro ornamentation is by Nicola Giuli (1762). The pendetives of the cupola, with images of the Four Evangelists are by Giovanni Andrea Carlone (1668) who also painted the frescoes in the apse and in the Bigazzini Chapel (1668-69) and in the Chapel of the Presentation of Mary (second on the left) which is, unfortunately, much re-painted. The paintings in the cupola, depicting the Coronation of Mary, are the work of Francesco Mancini from the Marches region of Italy (1728-1730). The frescoes in the north transept are by the Perugian artists, Giacinto Boccanera and Paolo Brizi (1735); those in the south transept are by Sebastiano Ceccarini of Urbino and Paolo Brizi (1737). The first chapel on the southside (dedicated to the Visitation of Mary) is decorated

The Church of St. Philip Neri: the Dome (18th century)

with frescoes by Vincenzo Monotti and Girolamo Perugini (1776) and has, above the altar, a canvas by Giuseppe Passeri of Rome (1709); the second (the Chapel of the Purification) has frescoes by Bernardino Gagliardi (1649) and was once host to the fine canvas by Andrea Sacchi (1631), today preserved in the Umbrian National Gallery; the third (the Chapel of the Assumption), with frescoes by Anton Maria Fabrizi (1636-1637), was built to a design by Marascelli between 1635 and 1637. Above the altar, there used to be the original of the Assumption by Guido Reni, today in the museum of Lyon (1637 circa). The canvas we see today is the work of Giovan Francesco Romanelli (17th century). The altar of the south transept was designed by Tommaso Stati (1652) and has a copy of an original by Guido Reni. Behind the main-altar which was also designed by Stati (1645), there hangs a large painting of the Conception of Mary by Pietro da Cortona (1662) with the probable collaboration of his pupils. The curve of the apse contains two paintings depicting St. John and St. Gregory by Pietro Montanini (1674), painted for the Church of St. Philip in memory of the unification of the two parishes of St. John Rotonda and St. Gregory the Great. The altar of the north transept has a precious bronze crucifix by Pasquale Pasqualini from Vianza (1685). Going back into the nave, the third chapel of the left (dedicated to the Birth of Our Lady), is decorated with frescoes by Anton Maria Fabrizi (1642). Above the altar, there used to be a Nativity by Pietro da Cortona, now in the Umbrian National Gallery. There now hangs a canvas by Simeone Ciburri depicting the Stigmata of St. Francis; the second chapel (of the Presentation of Mary), is adorned with frescoes by Giovanni Andrea Carlone and once displayed a canvas by Luigi Scaramuccia (also in the Gallery) which has now been replaced by a painting by Ulisse Ribustini; the first chapel (of the Annunciation), with frescoes by Vincenzo Monotti and Girolamo Perugini (1766) has, above the altar, a fine work by Francesco Trevisani (1710).

The Sacristy has a ceiling decorated by V. Carattoli and F. Appiani (18th century). It contains an oil painting by Vincenzo Pellegrini, alias the «Pittor Bello», representing the Conception with Archan-gel Michael and Mary Magdalen together with two small copper figures by Pietro Montanini (unfortunately stolen). Taking the nearby Via della Stella we arrive at the *Oratory of St. Cecilia* of the Philipian Fathers, an important example of Baroque archtecture in the round, designed by Pietro Baglioni (1690).

Continuing along Via dei Priori, on the left (no. 84), is the palazzo Marini Clarelli of the Oddi family with its 18th-century façade. A short distance further ahead, we come to the **Church of SS. Stephen and Valentine**. To be exact, the church whose apse and bell-tower are visible form the piazza is St. Stephen's, mentioned in documents as early as 1163 and certainly a parish church in 1285. It was enlarged during the 14th century with Gothic additions and restored at the beginning of this century. The title of St. Valentine was added in 1819 when this parish church was suppressed.

Inside, above the altar, there is a polyptych by Giustino Cristofani, made in 1911 after the style of the Quattrocento. On the far wall is a canvas depicting the enthroned Madonna and Saint in the style of Domenico Alfani (16th century). The walls show traces of frescoes from the 14th and early 15th centuries among these, the Archangel Michael and St. Catherine are of particular interest; they are fragments of a mural polyptych attributed to the Maestro Ironico (early 14th century). Above this, on the right, is an unattached 17th-century fresco depicting God the Father and Christ in glory among the Saints.

The Church of St. Theresa

On the left, is the **Church of St. Theresa of the Scalzi** (Barefoot). This was the seat of the Barefoot Carmelite sisters up to 1889. Its construction was completed in 1718 to a design by Alessandro Baglioni; the façade is unfinished and the arrangement of the church follows the Greek Cross with a dome in the centre and smaller cupola on the four sides.

The first altar on the right has a painting depicting St. Mary Magdelen of the Mad in glorious ecstacy and St. Luis Gonzaga by Anton Maria Garbi (18th century); to the right of this altar is an Annun-

The Church of St. Theresa and the Sciri Tower

ciation attributed to Ippolito Borghesi (17th century). The altar of the south transept, decorated in black, red and multicoloured marble, has stucco relief work and paintings by Giacinto Boccanera. It also contained the canvas by Francesco Mancini, today in the Umbrian Gallery (1732). The last altar on the right has an oil painting — the Virgin and Child between SS. Theresa and Joseph — by Gio-

vanni Antonio Scaramuccia (1632 circa). Left of the main altar, above the Sacristy door, is a painting of St. Joseph by Anton Maria Garbi. Above the altar of the north transept is a large canvas taken from the Laparelli Presbytery (18th century) depicting St. Theresa transfixed by the Angel, the Madonna and Child among the angels with the lower part taken up by St. John the Baptist, St. Antony of Padua, St. Peter, St. Francis of Paola and an angel carving the coat-of-arms of the Cesari family who were the proprietors of the altar. The next altar has a copy of Annibale Carracci's Deposition by A. M. Garbi. On the left is a fine Crucifix in carved multicoloured wood dating back to the 17th century.

Taking Via S. Stefano, we arrive at the **Church of St. Mary of the Francolini**, the façade of which is in Via Francolini. This church already existed in 1166 and was definitely a parish church by 1285; its parish status was transferred to the Church of St. Valentine in 1771; in 1779, it was donated to the 'Servants' of St. Anne. It was renovated in 1580 and rebuilt in 1792 to a design by Alessio Lorenzini. Inside, there are paintings ranging from the 16th to 18th centuries. Above the altar is a canvas by A.M. Garbi which depicts the Virgin, St. Anne and St. Joachine. The famous Perugian judge, Bartolo da Sassoferrato (+ Perugia, 1357) lived in the area of this parish. Further ahead, in Via Vincioli, on the corner with Piazza degli Offici, in the **House of the Missionary Fathers** (now the headquarters of the Finance Office), built in 1755 to a design by Pietro Carattoli.

Proceeding along Via dei Priori, on the left, we come to the famous *Sciri Tower*, the only remaining tower of the numerous ones which must have existed in Perugia. It is 46 metres high and takes its name from the Sciri family — one of the member families of the ruling oligarchy. (In fact, there are other towers still to be seen in Perugia, but they are generally hidden by and incorporated into other buildings). the tower is annexed to a religious institution founded in 1680 by Lucia Tartaglini of Cortona, a Franciscan Tertiary, in order to care for young girls. Today, it is used by the Oblate Sisters and the nuns of St. Philip Neri.

The Oratory of St. Francis

Turning into Via degli Sciri, at no. 6, we find the **Oratory of St. Francis**. The Franciscan brotherhood established itself here in 1319-20. In 1472, it formed a 'confederacy' with the Augustinian and Dominican Brotherhoods: the three orders united with eachother although each retained its own autonomy. The Historical Archives of all three are preserved here (the Braccio Fortebracci Archive). In 1890, they became a Religious Association for mutual aid among the Perugian nobility. These fraternities which had been originally composed of members from different social classes gradually began to restrict their membership to those of noble birth as the gradual process of aristocratic prevalence took hold of Perugia.

The vault of the atrium is decorated with stucco-work by the Frenchman, Jean Regnaud de Champagne (1675-76). In the friars' room, there is a portrait of Braccio Fortebracci (16th century). There is also an architectural relief in wood bearing the names of the Friars (17th century) as well as a 16th-century ballot box. The Oratory is among the most interesting and complete examples of Perugian early-Baroque art and has seats in walnut which were carved by the Perugians, Marco Pace and Sciarra Bovarelli (1584). The prior's seat (1585) and that of the Chairman (1604), are the work of Giampietro Zuccari of Sant'Angelo in Vado who also made the gold-plated frames of several paintings in the Oratory (1618-20). Other frames were made by the Germans, George Rachele of Boeslavia and Stefen Stobe of Regimont (1620). The box ceiling, carved and gold-plated, is the work of Girolamo di Marco, alias the 'Veneziano', and Maestro Ercole (1570-1574). The altar piece showing the Ascension of Christ is by the Mannerist painter, Leonardo after the style of Michael Angelo (1558). The two works on either side are by the Perugian artist. Paolo Gismondi, a discipline of Pietro da Cortona (1665). On the opposite wall, the paintings of St. Augustine and St. Domenic are by Bernardino Gagliardi (1657). The series of paintings on the theme of Mary and Christ (The Annunciation, Visitation, Nativity, Adoration of the Magi, Presentation in the Temple, Flight into Egypt, the Discussion with the Learned Doctors and the Resurrection) is the most important pictorial ensemble of the Perugian artist, Giovanni Antonio Scaramuccia, painted between 1611 and 1425, except for the Resurrection (1627). In the Sacristy, along with several pieces of liturgical furniture and instruments, is the splendid processional banner of the Brotherhood depicting the Flagellation of Christ by Pietro di Galeotto of Perugia (1480).

The Oratory of St. Francis (17th century)

Giovanni da Sciampagna: Stucco-work in the atrium (17th century)

**Pietro di Galeotto: The Flegellation
(15th century)**

Going back into Via dei Priori, immediately on the left, is the **Church of the Madonna of Light** which was begun in 1513 to honour the miraculous image of the Virgin. The elegant Renaissance façade is attributed to various different architects (Cesario del Roscetto? Giulio Danti?). Inside, there is a fresco by Tiberio of Assisi representing Our Lady between St. Francis and St. Ludovic. The frescoes in the cupola are the work of Giovanni Battista Caporali (1532) and depict the Eternal Father in glory.

At the beginning of the steps of Via del Piscinello, we can observe the **Etruscan Doorway** or **Porta S. Luca** (due to its proximity to the church of St. Luke), sometimes called the Trasimeno doorway as it represents the beginning of the road which leads to Lake Trasimeno and Tuscany. The pointed archway was rebuilt during Mediaeval times.

From here, we can go up the staircase and turn into Via della Sposa; towards the end of this road, on the right, we come to the **Church of St. Andrew**, already a parish church in 1285; a short way further ahead is the mediaeval **door** of **St. Susanna**. We can continue along the Piaggia

The Church of the Madonna of Light and of St. Luke (16th century)

The Trasimeno or St. Luke's Gate

Colombata to the **Church of St. Mary of the Colombata** (or Colomata) of which remains the red and white stone façade with its charming gothic doorway. Inside, there are traces of 14th-century frescoes. It was the seat of a community of Benedictine nuns from the end of the 1200's onwards; in 1437, it was closed down because of the licentiousness of the nuns; other nuns resided there during the 15th and 16th centuries but, perhaps because of its position outside the town walls, the place never had a stable community.

Next door to the Church of the Madonna of Light, is the **Church of St. Luke**, a mediaeval parish church; it belonged to the Knights of Malta from 1560 circa. It was modified into its present form in 1586, following a plan attributed to Bino Sozi. Inside, there is a canvas depicting the Virgin Mary, St. John the Baptist and St. Luke by Giovanni Antonio Scaramuccia (1632). One of the chapels contains an image of Our Lady of Grace, perhaps a copy of a 14th-century original.

Next to this church is the **Casa della Commenda**, built in the 15th-century architectural style with crossed windows similar to those of the Old University building.

71

The Church of St. Francis: façade and north flank

The Church of St. Francis

At the end of Via S. Francesco, we come to a piazza dominated by the church of St. Francis al Prato at the side of which, on the left, stands the Oratory of St. Bernardino; a short way ahead, on the right, is the small church of St. Matthew in Campo d'Oro.

Franciscan Minors were already present in Perugia, certainly by 1230, residing at first in the *Pástina* locality, a zone oppo-

site the present church and monastery. In 1253, the friars sold this site together with the structures built on it, to the Benedictine nuns of St. Angelo del Renaio (a convent outside Perugia) for the sum of 2,000 lire, in order to invest in a «loco novo beati Francisi de Perusio posito in Campo de orto» («a new site for the Perugian Franciscans in the Campo d'orto»). The place which they left and to which the nuns moved, took on the title of St. Francis of the Women (see further on). Between 1248 and 1256, the Franciscans secceeded in obtaining the area of St. Matthew in Campo d'Orto which had belonged to the Monastery of Santa Croce of Fonte Avallana. From this time on, the Minors had a stable community; they built the aisleless church with a transept and polygon-shaped apse. This new church attracted a large congregating many of whom often chose to be buried there or to leave money to the friars. Among those buried there, are the Judge, Bartolo da Sassoferrato and the Mercenary, Braccio Fortebracci. Various aristocratic families aspired to built here their private chapels and sepulchral monuments. With the division of the Franciscan Order into Conventuals and Observants, St. Francis al Prato became (and is still) the seat of the Conventuals while the Observants moved to Monteripido (St. Francis of the Mount).

The church is no longer consecrated and has undergone radical transformations — particularly inside — due to numerous efforts throughout the centuries to prevent the ruination of the walls which stand on unstable terrain. As early

as the 1400's, Braccio Fortebracci had consulted architects from Perugia, Siena, Arezzo and even France about the possibility of re-enforcing the church. In the 18th century, another attempt was made under the supervision of Pietro Carattoli (1740 circa). He demolished the defective vaulting and lowered the walls by about two metres (a recent restoration has taken them back to their original height) in order to re-enforce the interior of the walls upon which he placed a Roman type vault and a dome. The sliding movement of the land again rendered the benefits of this renovation transitory to the extent that, only a century later, it was necessary to demolish the dome and vaulting of the nave and transept and part of the walls of the apse. In 1926, a new project was begun, consisting of the renovation on the façade, which had been freed of a large block of apartments which had been built in the 1700's, and the renewal of parts of the side walls. However, these works were soon suspended to be re-commenced in 1960, adopting new techniques which, above all, served to arrest the subsidence of the land. On the left side of the Church is the

The Academy of Fine Arts: plaster cast collection

Chapel of the Conception or of the Banner, built around the mid-1400's and overlaid with pink panels. It contains the banner of Benedetto Bonfigli (1464), made in memory of the great plague, the tomb of Braccio Fortebracci and the tomb of Bartolo da Sassoferrato. The red stone altar dates from the 15th century. The fine wrought iron gate dates from the same period. The church's interior, today completely stripped of its ancient furnishings, used to be host to numerous masterpieces, now to be seen in the Umbrian National Gallery or in national and foreign private collections. Among these, the works of greatest interst are the following: the Deposition by Baglioni di Raffaello, today in the Borghese Gallery in Rome, the Incoronation of the Virgin, also by Raffaello, now in the Vatican Gallery, the Marriage of St. Catherine by Orazio Alfani, currently in the Louvre, and the Resurrection by Pietro Perugino, also in the Vatican Panoteque.

Next to the Oratory of St. Bernardino, is the entrance to the **Academy of Fine Arts,** named after Pietro Vannucci; this, together with the State Institute of Art, occupies the rooms of the former monastery of St. Francis. In the second cloister (the first, designed by Pietro Carattoli has been demolished) there are still visible some lunettes painted by early-17th century artists from Assisi.

The Academy of Fine Arts, founded in 1573 by Orazio Alfani and Domenico Sozi, established itself in the monastery of St. Francis al Prato towards the beginning of this century. Previously, it had resided in the Church of St. Angelo della Pace, near porta Sole, and in the convent of Monte Morcino Nuovo. Its important art collection comprises a rich collection of plaster casts (about 500) including a group by Antonio Canova representing the Three Graces (1822), a plaster replica of the one made for the duke of Bedford; the Shepherd by Thorswalden (1832); the

The Academy of Fine Arts: picture room - Agostino Carracci (?) Landscape (17th century)

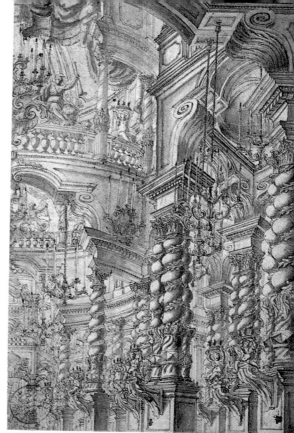

Academy of Fine Arts: Drawing studio, by a student of Jacque Callot, Group of Figures
(17th century); Giuseppe Galli (alias the «Bibiena»), Stage set (18th century)
Academy of Fine Arts: the Museum of the «Ottocento», Domenico Bruschi, A Sketch (19th century)

four casts after the style of Michael Angelo representing Dawn, Twilight, Day and Night, copied from the originals by Vincenzo Danti (or, as some say, by Michael Angelo himself); there is a collection of paintings, mainly by 19th-century Perugian artists (Gaspare, Sensi, Giuseppe Rossi, Napoleone Verga, Guglielmo Mangiarelli, Matteo Tassi, Mariano Guardabassi, Domenico Bruschi, Annibale Brugnoli, etc.); and a conspicuous selection of drawings and engravings ranging from the 16th to 19th centuries.

The Oratory of St. Bernardino

St. Bernardino of Siena preached in Perugia in 1425, 1438 and 1441; in 1444, he passed through the city but probably did not preach owing to his declining health.

His much-felt impression on Perugian life is apparent in the reform of its statutes (*Statuta Bernardiana*) and in the widespread devotion to the name of Jesus, as demonstrated in the trigram IHS, engraved above numerous doorways. Immediately after his canonisation (1450), in 1451, the priors of Perugia decided to honour his memory by building a chapel; thus, the **Oratory of St. Bernardino** was constructed, so admired today for its façade attributed to the Florentine, Agostino di Antonio di Duccio (1457 to 1461). Two lateral pilasters sustain a tympanum and outline the median area which has a twin door above which is a huge lunette. On the tympanum, is a sculpture of Christ among the angels. The words '*Augusta Perusia MCCCCLXI*' are inscribed on the cornice. In the upper niches, on the left, is a statue of Archangel Gabriel and,

The Piazza of St. Francis al Prato.

Agostino di Duccio, details of St. Bernardino Oratory façade: the Glory of St. Bernardino; the Holy Bishop; Musician Angels

The Tomb of the Blessed Egidio (15th century)

beneath, there is a bas-relief depicting the Saint welcoming Giacomo della Marca to the Franciscan Order; on the right, is an Annunciation beneath which there is a bas-relief showing the miracle of the star which appeared above the head of the Saint when he was preaching in Aquila; the lower niches contain statues of St. Costanzo and St. Herculanus (the two patron Bishops of the city) together with St. Lawrence. Beneath them, there is a griffin, the emblem of Perugia. The lunette shows St. Bernardino ascending into the sky amidst angel musicians and cherubs. Below this, divided into three sections, is a panel showing three episodes from the life of the Saint: on the right, a miracle which occurred in Aquila shortly after the death of the Saint; in the centre, we see St. Bernardino preaching to the people of Perugia; on the left, two children are saved form drowing by intercession of the Saint. Below these scenes, is the inscription — «*Opus Augustini Florentini lapicidae*». On the inner-sides of the doorway, the six Virtues are represented (Religion, Mortification, Pentience, Mercy, Devotion and Purity); towards the exterior are six groups of angel musicians. The interior of the Oratory is Gothic is form: three sections with a cross-vault. On the right-hand wall there is a copy of the Deposition by Raffaello Baglioni, painted by Orazio Alfani (17th century). The altar is

a paleo-Christian tomb in which the body of the Blessed Egidio was placed in 1494. In type, it conforms to the 'columned' sarcophagus style in so far as the front of the cask is divided by columns into niches. In the central niche is the figure of Christ sitting on a throne; on the left, there is a female figure holding a *scroll*; on the right, there is an old bearded man also holding a *scroll*. Beginning from the left, the first niche contains an old man perhaps in the act of preaching, the second contains a young man reading a *scroll*. From the right, the first niche has an old man with a *scroll* at his feet; in the second, there is the figure of a young man with a rolled up *scroll* at his feet. The meaning of this tomb front is by no means clear. On either side of the lid, there are two male figures (St. Peter? St. Paul?). Left of the *dedicatory tablet* is the figure of Noah waiting to receive the dove and Jonah, thrown out of the belly of the whale; on the right is the scene of Jonah being thrown into the sea. The scenes from the story of Jonah could symbolise the Christian hope of Resurrection. The sarcophagus is attributed to the workshop of Giunio Basso (late 14th century).

Next to the Oratory of St. Bernardino is the **Oratory of SS. Andrew and Bernardino**, also called the Oratory of Justice. The Brotherhood of St. Andrew was formed in 1374 and first resided in the little church of St. Mustiola, a dependent of the Canons of the Church of St. Mustiola in Chiusi. One of the chief functions of the Brotherhood was to give spiritual aid to those condemned to death from which it took on the name of the Brotherhood of Justice. In 1537, it merged with the Brotherhood of St. Bernardino, founded between 1456 and 1460. In the same year, the Brotherhood was given the site near the Church of St. Maria dell'Oliveto, near porta St. Pietro. After this, the present Oratory was built.

We enter the church through a small atrium. On the walls, from right to left, there is a Sermon of St. John the Baptist painted by Marcello Leopardi (1787), a Miracle of St. Bernardino by Carlo Labruzzi (1787) and St. Andrew threatened with floggin by Marcello Leopardi (1785). The altar was carved in 1629 and gold-plated by Giacomo Agretti in 1762. On the right, there is a canvas depicting the Baptism of Jesus also by Leopardi (1781). The altar is host to a canvas by Gaetano Lapis (1762) depicting the Virgin and Child with St. John the Baptist, St. An-

drew and St. Bernardino. Left of the altar is a painting by Marcello Leopardo representing the Decapitation of St. John the Baptist, again by Leopardi (1783). The inner-façade wall has, on the right, a painting of St. Andrew embracing the Cross of his Martyrdom by Vincenzo Ferreri (1790); on the left, St. Bernardino refuses to become a Cardinal, also by Ferreri (1790). The multicoloured marble floor and the walnut pews were made between 1817 and 1818. The box-vaulted ceiling was gold-plated and carved in 1588.

Next to the Church of St. Francis, on the right, is the **Church of St. Matthew in Campo d'Orto** with its trapezoidal bell-tower which was transferred here from the demolished Church of St. Mary of Verzaro. This church was the property of the Monastery of S. Croce at Fonte Avellana until its definitive concession to the Franciscan Minors (1256). In front of the Church of St. Francis, we observe the fine arch by Valentino Martelli which was originally located infront of the entrance of the Old University (in Piazza Matteotti).

From the Church of St. Francis, we

Oratory of Ss. Bernardino and Andrew or of Justice

proceed along Via Alessandro Pascoli. We can deviate into Via dell'Eremita, reaching as far as the small piazza in which the **Church of SS. Sebastian and Rocco** is situated. This church took on parochial status when the Church of St. Elizabeth was demolished.

This area of the city is known as the «Conca» (basin) on account of its position between the elevated areas of Verzaro and porta St. Angelo. Around the beginning of the 13th century this area, which belonged to the Cathedral, began to become populated, taking on the characteristics of a 'borgo' (quarter) whilst maintaining its surrounding fields and orchards. Thus, we have another example of mediaeval urban expansion: in fact, where the ends of Via Goldoni and Via del Maneggio meet, we find the old Conca Gateway, built entirely in travertine rock; at the end of Via A. Pascoli, we find the 'new' Conca Gateway with its mediaeval wall, erected during the first half of the 14th century.

A pre-existing chapel had been given to the Brotherhood of St. Sebastian in 1484;

A Roman Mosaic (200 A.D.)

in the early 1500's, after a miraculous event attributed to the image of the Madonna of the Milk (15th century), which can still be seen inside, the small church was enlarged and took on the name of Madonna della Pace (of Peace). From the mid-1600's on, a community of hermits resided behind the oratory; amongst these Francesco Van-Outers from Brussels who died in 1729.

The internal walls have frescoes by Pietro Montanini representing episodes from the lives of SS. Sebastian and Rocco, scenes from the Day of Judgement and pictures of St. John in the Desert and St. Onofrio (1665 circa). The paintings on the box ceiling and in the Presbytery (beyond the wrought iron grille) are the work of Giovan Francesco Bassotti (1665). In the right-hand chapel there is a canvas showing scenes from the life of St. Onofrio attributed to Pietro Montanini (1672), taken from the Dyers' altar in the nearby Church of St. Elizabeth.

From Via dell'Eremita, taking Via St. Sebastian, we arrive in Via S. Elisabetta, infront of the Faculty of Chemistry. Here, beyond the outer walls of the now demolished parish Church of St. Elizabeth (1337 circa), there is a large mosaic dating back to the 11th century, possibly part of a thermal complex, which depicts Orpheus pursued by the furies.

On reaching the Conca Gateway at the end of Via A. Pascoli, we turn into Via St. Galgano. On the left, we see the Dyers' Fountain, erected in 1388. The dyers' trade was one of the most widespread among the inhabitants of the Conca. Taking the communal road of S. Lucia, still on the left, we reach the ancient **fountains of St. Galgano**. In 1279, a Benedictine convent was already established here. In 1412, it merged with the convent of St. Francis of the Women. The area possessed natural springs which were thought to have healing powers. In 1635-40, a thermal bath was built here. After the Unification, in 1862, a company was formed to exploit the potential of the said springs. From the beginning of the 1900's, the spring of St. Galgano began to fall into disuse. Continuing along this road, we ascend the hill of **Monte Morcino Vecchio** where, in 1366, in accordance with the wishes of Cardinal Nicolò Capocci, a community of Olivetans was founded which was destined to remain there until 1740, when the construction of the 'New' Monastery of Monte Morcino was begun. A few 14th-century remnants of the monastic buildings are still visible. They are thought to be the work of Francesco di Guido of Settignano.

The 'New' Monastery of Monte Morcino

From Via S. Elisabetta we turn into a stretch of Via dell'Elce di sotto, the end of which is marked by a mediaeval gateway of the same name. From here, we take Via Aurora or, further ahead, Via del Liceo, both leading into Via Fabretti. Proceeding to the left, we come to the Piazza dell'Università. The vast building which today house offices, institutes and the University Central Library, was originally a huge 18th-century religious complex. The Olivetan monks of the 'Old' Monastery of Monte Morcino moved here in 1740 in order to have at their disposal a larger and more convenient building. The vast monastic complex was entitled **Monte Morcino Nuovo** (the New) and was designed by Carlo Murena; Luigi Vanvitelli designed the Neoclassical style church. In

The Church of Monte Morcino Nuovo (18th century)

1811, the French Government assigned the building to the University. One section of the large cloister contains a collection of casts taken of Etruscan inscriptions donated to the University by Count Giancarlo Conestabile in 1860.

Continuing along Via F. Innamorati and then a stretch of Via Z. Faina, we reach the **former Monastery of St. Francis of the Women** which was probably Perugia's first Franciscan community; it was taken over by the Benedictine nuns of Angelo del Renaio (see further back - St. Francis al Prato), who remained here up to 1815, the year in which the convent was suppressed; it was then converted to secular use.

On the return journey from the Conca, we can reach the town centre by climbing the steps of Via Appia. Of particular note are the arches — restored in 1516 by Vincenzo Danti — of the aqueduct which was built during the second half of the 13th century, transporting water from Monte Pacciano to the famous fountain.

Almost at the end of Via Appia, we can see the Etruscan Arch of which only a few gothic remains are left.

Here, we find ourselves in Via Baldeschi and directly on our left is Piazza Cavallotti with its 16th-century Palazzo Baldeschi.

From Piazza Cavallotti, we can turn into the characteristic Via del Verzaro. At

The Church of St. Martino of Verzaro: Giannicola di Paolo (?), Madonna and Child with Saints (16th century)

Via Appia.

the beginning, no. 3, closed in between the buildings, is a typical mediaeval tower. A few yeards ahead, we come to the **Church of St. Martin of Verzaro**, today an Encumenical Centre; this building dates back to before 1163; it was partly dependent on the Canons of the Cathedral and partly on the Monastery of St. Angelo of Chiaserra (Diocese of Gubbio). In 1257, the Abbot of St. Angelo turned his part over to the Monastery of St. Jiuliana in Perugia. In 1285, it became a parish church and continued to belong to the Cathedral Charter until the end of the 1500's. It is an aisleless church with a small trapezoidal bell-tower. Inside, on the wall behind the altar, there are frescoes attributed to Giannicola di Paolo (Virgin and Child, St. Lawrence and St. John): the right-hand section of the far wall depicts the scene in which St. Martin gives half his cloak to a beggar, by a Perugian artist; the left-hand section shows the

Crucifixion with Mary Magdalen, Our Lady and St. John by a Mannerist artist.

Going back down Via del Verzaro, still on the right, is Piazza Morlacchi, dominated by an attractive 18th-century building, today the seat of the Faculty of Letters; next to this is the **Communal Francesco Morlacchi Theatre**, built in 1778-80 on the innitiative of the new up-and-coming bourgeoisie who wished to emulate the nobility which had financed the construction of the Pavone Theatre (see further on). The architect was the Perugian, Alessio Lorenzini; the theatre was restored in 1874 and was dedicated to Perugia's most famous musician. Opposite the theatre is the Palazzo Bianchi, begun in 1873 and built to a design by Guglielmo Calderini; it is a good example of Perugian bourgeois architecture.

The Maestà delle Volte
(Her Majesty of the Vaults)

From Piazza Cavallotti, we return to Piazza Grande taking the Via Maestà delle Volte. This was the dark Mediaeval thoroughfare in which the votive image of the Virgin and Child was painted in 1297. In front of this image a lamp shone continuously. After a while, in recognition of the devotion of the people, a church was built; among those who worked on the façade, was Agostino di Antonio di Duccio (some of his sculptures are exhibited in the Umbrian National Gallery). The area suffered extensive damage during a fire in 1534. In 1566, the 'jus patronatus' of the church passed from the city to the seminary. Between 1580 and 1590, the church took on its present form which was based on a plan by Bino Sozi. The church has now been converted into a shop for religious ornaments. However, it still contains ancient frescoes (much-repainted) whose unknown author is traditionally referred to as the 'Maestro della Maestà delle Volte'. The frescoes in the vault are signed by Nicolò Circignani, the so-called 'Pomarancio' (1568). On the left is a fine arch, built in red and white marble; it is probably a remnant of a 14th-century portico; on the right is a modern work depicting the Virgin of the Maestà delle Volte by G. Belletti (1945). The fountain in a hollow beneath the church is by the architect, Pietro Angelini (1929).

The Maestà delle Volte

The Maestà delle Volte, mediaeval archway.

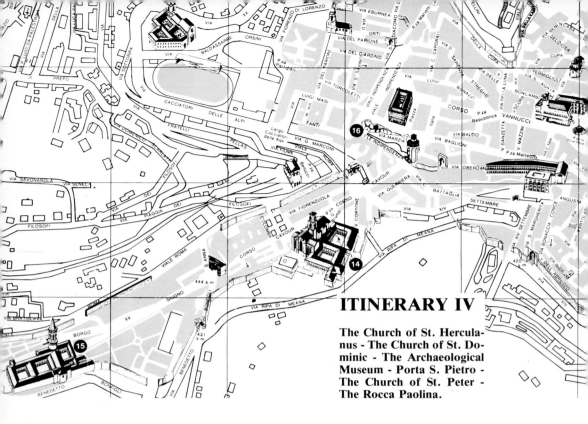

ITINERARY IV

The Church of St. Hercula-
nus - The Church of St. Do-
minic - The Archaeological
Museum - Porta S. Pietro -
The Church of St. Peter -
The Rocca Paolina.

From Piazza Matteotti we turn into Via Oberdan. Part of this road was occupied by the **Hospice of St. Mary of Mercy** (della Misericordia) and its connected church. Its engraved emblem is still visible at nos. 40 and 58 (a trigram consisting of the uncial letters *d, m, e* = domus Misericordie).

In 1296, the Brotherhood of Mercy had already existed for sometime, composed of clerics and laymen; however, it was in 1305 that the Bishop of Perugia officially recognised the foundation of the Hospice of St. Mary of Mercy to accomodate pilgrims, the poor and infirm and abandoned children. From this time on, it developed into the most important charity and welfare institution in the city. From 1862, it was run by the Perugian Congregation of Charity. At no. 54, we can see the door of the church which was renovated in 1760 to a design by Pietro Carattoli. On the left, there is a large niche containing a figure of Our Lady of Mercy attributed to Giovan Battista Caporali (16th century); on the right, a small niche contains a Madonna between two angels attributed to Martino da Perugia (14th century).

Descending the St. Herculanus stair-

case, before reaching the church, we come across a gate called the **arch of St. Hercu-lanus** (or the Cornea or Berarda Arch), the lower area of which is Etruscan while the arch is decidely Gothic.

The Church of St. Herculanus

The **Church of St. Herculanus** — the 'defensor civitas' Bishop, symbol of the city's municipal autonomy — was built during the first decades of the 14th century. It had the form of a polygon shaped tower and was originally composed of two separate levels. The upper level (with its entrance in the present-day Via Marzia) was destroyed after the construction of the Rocca Paolina in order to afford a better view of the valley. In 1607, Bishop Napoleon Comitoli sponsored a renovation of the building which had already begun in 1604, with the construction of the double-flighted staircase replacing the old semi-circular one built out of the stones taken from the 13th-century Arnolfo Fountain. Inside, the cupola and lunettes are painted with scenes from the life of St. Paul by Giovanni Andrea Carlone from

The Garden and Church of St. Herculanus

The Church of St. Hercolanus and the Berarda Gate

Genoa (1675). The monochrome gold-finished decorations are by Nicola Giuli. On the right, is the Chapel of St. Charles Borromeo containing stucco-work (1682) by the Frenchman, Jean Regnaud (Giovanni di Sciampagna) who also did the stucco-work in the opposite Chapel of St. Martin. The altar-piece of this Chapel shows a Miracle worked by St. Martin and is attributed to Anton Maria Garbi. The central area of the apse is occupied by a copy of Pietro Perugino's Decemvir altar-piece, perhaps by Biagio di Angelo. On each side there is a painting by Giovanni Andrea Carlone (St. Peter and St. Paul) and two paintings (four in all) by Mattia Salvucci showing episodes from the life of St. Herculanus (1627 circa). The main altar is composed of a fine 4th-century sarcophagus, discovered in 1609 in the Church of St. Orfito near Perugia. The Sacristy contains a canvas depicting Mary as a Child, St. Anne and St. Joachine by Anton Maria Garbi (18th century).

At the end of the staircase of St. Herculanus, we turn left into Corso Cavour. This was one of the main street which lin-

The Church of St. Hercolanus and the Berarda Gate

85

ked the old city to the great Abbey of St. Peter and the Church of St. Costanzo; it was also the beginning of the road leading to Assisi and Rome. On the right, on the corner with Via Marconi, we see the ancient **Church of S. Croce** which used to belong to the Knights of the Holy Sepulchre from the late 1100's. Towards the end of the 19th century, it was taken over by Company of St. Joseph of the Carpenters, founded in 1577 by a master carpenter. It thus takes its present name of St. Joseph's from this company. Its interior contains an unattached much-repainted early 15th-century fresco, depicting Our Lady of Mercy. On the left, there is a canvas showing Our Lady between SS. Joseph and Claud by Giovanni Antonio Scaramuccia (1632 circa); on the right is another canvas emulating the style of Ludovico Carracci, possibly by Luigi Scaramuccia (17th century).

The Church of St. Dominic

From here, we proceed ahead until we reach Piazza Giordano Bruno which is dominated by the imposing structure of the **Church of St. Dominic**. Of interest is the piazza's fine well-curb dating 1452. During the early Middle Ages, this area was the site of the local horse market and fair.

The Dominican Order was admitted to this area in 1234, at which time it was still part of the parish of St. Stephen of Castellare, listed in the Cathedral Charter sometime before 1163. In 1304, the parish was definitively conceded to the Preaching friars by Benedict XI in order to extend the Church of St. Dominic. The same Pope later granted a plenary indulgence to this church for having claimed to contain the body of St. Stephen the Martyr, obviously in competition with the

The Church of St. Domenic   **The window in the apse (15th century)** ▶

Porziuncola in Assisi. After 1437, the Monastery of St. Dominic passed into the hands of the Observants; it became the seat of a *Studium* and, during the 1400's was elevated to the rank of '*Studium solemne*'.

Tradition has it that the church was designed by Giovanni Pisano. In any case, its construction was completed in 1458, the year in which it was consecrated to St. Stephen by Pope Pius II. Before the 17th-century renovation of the interior (by Carlo Maderno - 1632), the building presented an enormous 'hallenkirche' plan with octogonal pilasters in laterite stone, pointed arches and large stained-glass windows. The bell-tower was once surmonted by a high steeple dating from the late 1400's and was the work of Gasperino di Antonio of Lombardy. It was shortened during the 15th century, probably for reasons of instability, although tradition identifies in this act the same motivations which prompted Pope Paul III to demolish the upper level of the church of St. Herculanus. The front staircase was designed by Girolamo Ciofi of Cortona (1640). The doorway is dated 1596. Above

it remain traces of a rose-window by Benedetto di Valdorcia of Siena (1415).

The interior, once rich with precious furnishings (many of which are preserved in the Umbrian National Gallery) has, on the far wall, a fresco by Anton Maria Fabrizi depicting the Virgin and child between SS. Dominic, Catherine of Siena, Costanzo and Herculanus and a group of Kneeling disciples; it was painted in 1656 in memory of the Great Plague. The first chapel of the south aisle (the Chapel of the Blessed Colomba of Rieti) has above the altar a copy of an original by Spagna, today preserved in the Umbrian National Gallery. The second (the Chapel of St. Rose of Lima) contains a canvas after the style of Maratto by Giuseppe Laudati showing the marriage of St. Rose of Lima to Jesus; the left-hand wall bears a Mystical Marriage of St. Catherine by the same artist whilst the right-hand wall has a painting by an anonimous 18th-century artist also depicting the Mystical Marriage of St. Rose of Lima. Above the altar of the third chapel (the Chapel of St. Pius V) is a painting of St. Pius V giving relics to the Ambassador of the King of Poland by

The Church of St. Domenic: Interior

Agostino di Duccio: the Angel of the Annunciation (15th century)

Giuseppe Laudati. The walls bear paintings depicting episodes from the life of Pius V by Mattia Batini and Giacinto Boccanera (18th century). The fourth Chapel (of St. Lawerence, today of the Votive Madonna), is still in the Gothic style. It contains the altar-frontal by Agostino di Antonio of Duccio (1459) in stone and white painted terracotta. It has the form of a large niche bordered by parastas with tabernacles and is surmounted by a trabeation with a lunette. The Florentine sculptor made the Madonna and angels in the lunette as well as the statues of St. John the Baptist and St. Lawrence in the tabernacles. The painted medallions in the triangles of the arch are by the Florentine, Bernardo di Girolamo Rosselli. In the sides of the arch, there are small squares depicting miracles attributed to the Rosary. The frescoes (1869) on background of the niches (the Glory of the Angels and SS. Stephen, Nicholas, Blessed Tommasello and Blessed Benedict XI) are work of Domenico Bruschi of Perugia.

The facing wall bears a large canvas depicting the Resurrection of Christ, a copy of a work by Annibale Carracci (by Giuseppe Laudati - 1718).

Following this, there is the former Chapel of St. Peter the Martyr, transformed during the 18th century into a side entrance to the church. In a niche on the right-hand wall, we find the sepulchral monument of Judge Guglielmo Pontano after the style of Sansovini (16th century). The south transept (at the head of which the Chapel of St. Domenic was built in 1450, similar to the Banner Chapel in St. Francis al Prato) contains two 18th-century canvases. The Chapel of St. Peter the Martyr (first on the right of the four chapels in the apse) contains a painting by Bonaventura Borghesi of Cortona (1705)

The Sepulchral Monument of Benedict XI (14th century)

89

Alessandro Algardi: the Bust of Elisabetta Cantucci (17th century)

depicting the Martyrdom of St. Peter together with remains of votive frescoes
from the 14th and 15th centuries. Next to
this, is the Chapel of the Apostles (now of
Blessed Benedict XI) with vault frescoes
depicting the various Dominican saints by
a late-gothic artist of the early 15th century. On the right-hand wall, is the sepulchral monument of Benedict XI (14th century) transferred here from the Church
of St. Domenic during the 18th century.
Structurally speaking, it resembles the
form of the sepulchtral monument of
Cardinal Guglielmo De Braye by Arnolfo
di Cambio in the Church of St. Domenic
in Orvieto (1282 circa) and it is tradition-

ally thought to be the work of Vasari and
Giovanni Pisano. However, its stylistic si-
milarities with the Cathedral of Orvieto
leads to the conclusion that, in fact, it is
the work of an Umbrian artist of the Tuscan school. The monument consists of a
shrine resting upon twisting columns with
marble tarsia-work and cherubs under-
which there is a canopy and the reposing
figure of the deceased; the sarcophagus is
surmonted by a plaque with figures of
saints and a mullioned-window with three
lights showing the Virgin, St. Domenic
and the kneeling Pope. On the column se-
parating this chapel from the apse, there
is the tomb of Elizabeth Cantucci de Colis

90

with a valuable bust by Alessandro Algardi (1648); on the opposite column is the sepulchral monument of the prelate Alessandro Benincasa with a marble bust by Domenico Guidi (1594). The main altar, begun in 1720 to a design by Pietro Carattoli, was completed in a successive epoch and in a style not entirely in keeping with the original plan. The apse remained completely unaffected by the 17th-century renovation works and has a large Renaissance Choir begun in 1476 by Crispolito da Bettona (the section on the left) with the help of Polimante della Spina and Giovanni Schiavo (the section on the right). The marquetry-work is by Antonio da Mercatello (1498). At the centre, there is a huge ogival window — one of the largest in Italy after the ones in Milan Cathedral — with stained-glass made in 1411 by the Perugian, Bartolomeo di Pietro and Mariotto di Nardi, a Florentine. The left-hand pillaster of the Presbytery is host to the sepulchral monument of the Danti family with a bush of Vincenzio, sculpted by Valerio Cioli (16th century). The next chapel (previously of St. Nicholas, now the Chapel of the Name of Jesus) has a painting of the Circumcision by Giuseppe Berettini (17th century), nephew and disciple of Pietro da Cortona. On the left, is the sepulchral monument of Bishop Benedetto Guidalotti (1429) attributed to Urban of Cortona. In 1437, to honour this family and its chapel, Beato Angelico painted a beautiful polyptych now preserved in the Umbrian National Gallery. The right-hand wall shows St. Ursula and the Virgins by Benedetto Bandiera (17th century). The four section of the vault bear frescoes by a Giottesque artist, recently identified as Allegretto Nuzi from the Marches region (14th century).

Next, is the Chapel of the Angel (now, of St. Thomas) with various votive frescoes including the Killing of St. Peter the Martyr attributed to Cola Petriccioli (late-14th century), a Martyrdom of St.

Cola Petruccioli (?): the Martyrdom of St. Peter (14th century)

**Giovanni Lanfranco: Madonna and Child
between SS. Domenic and Catherine
(17th century)**

Sebastian dating 1396 and a Madonna
and Child and St. Lucy dating 1370. The
altar-piece showing the Ecstasy of St.
Thomas is by Mattia Batini (18th
century). The head of the north transept
is occupied by the Great Organ by Sallu-
stio da Lucignano and Luca Neri da Leo-
nessa (second half of the 17th century).
The canvas depicting the Pentecost, enclosed within a 16th-century pietra serena
showcase, is the work of Sister Plantilla
Nelli da Pistoia (1554). The altar is flanked
by two doors — the one on the left leading
into the Sacristy — above which are hung
two canvases by Anton Maria Fabrizi (the
Martyrdom of St. Dorothy and St. Cecilia
and Valerian - 17th century).

The Sacristy is a large square-shaped
ambient, built in the 14th century and
modified in the 1700's. The centre of the
vault and the lunettes bear frescoes by
Mattia Battini. Along the walls are portraits of Popes and Cardinals of the Domenican Order; it also contains numerous
pieces of 18th-century furniture. A 17th-
century canvas by Benedetto Bandiera
hangs above the altar. A showcase built
into the wall contains belongings of Benedict XI (dalmatic, surplice, boots, scep-
tre, stole and slippers) all articles dating
from the 14th century.

Going back into the Church, the first
chapel in the north aisle (the Chapel of St.
Catherine), still in the Gothic style, contains numerous rather fragmented frescoes, said to be the work of Varsari di
Taddeo di Bartolo but more probably
that of Benedetto di Bindo and his pupils
(1415 circa). There follows: the Chapel of
the Resurrection or Rosary which has
above the altar a painting of the Madonna
and Child together with SS. Domenic and
Catherine of Siena by Giovanni Lanfranco (1647); the Banner Chapel, named after the Banner by Giannicola di Paolo
(1494), contained therein, depicting, in
the upper section Christ, with the Virgin
Mary, St. John and other saints, whilst
the lower sectin depicts a group of faithful between St. Domenic and the Blessed
Colomba, an interesting example of Perugian art of this period; the Chapel of St.
Vincent Ferreri, containing a canvas
(1730) by Francesco Busti and another representing St. Luke (1675 circa) by Giovanni Andrea Carlone; the Chapel of Our
Lady of Sorrows with a wooden Pietà dating from the 17th century after the style
of Micheal Angelo.

At no. 6, Piazza Giordano Bruno, we see
the entrance to the **cloister** of the monastery, one of the largest in the city with
fourty travertine columns. It was begun in
1455 and finished in 1589. One side of the
cloister incorporates the façade of the old
gothic Church of St. Dominic with its
twin portal in white and red stone. Beside
this, is a gate leading into another cloister
which contains the entrance to the **Perugian State Archives**, one of the richest in
Italy; it possesses important historical
sources regarding the city, amongst them
— *The Historical Archive of the Perugia
Commune* and the *Suppressed Religious
Associations*, as well as a cospicuous collection of notarial documents. The Archives occupies the rooms of the former monastery of St. Dominic which includes the

Giannicola di Paolo: a Banner section (16th century)

The Cloister of St. Domenic's: remnants of the façade of the Old Church of St. Domenic

Library Hall, a fifteenth century structure (1475-1481) divided into a nave and two aisles by travertine columns. The far wall bears a fresco — originally from the Monastery of Monteluce — depicting the Crucifixion (14th century).

The Archaeological Museum

The arcade is the home of the **Archaeological Museum**.

The Museum has its origins in a donation made by Francesco Filippo Friggeri who gave his valuable collection of Etruscan and Roman works to the city of Perugia in 1790. This collection was subsequently added to by donations from the following families: Oddi, Graziani, Ansidei, Guardabassi, Bellucci (amulets) and Antinori (African objects). After a brief spell in the Priors' Palace, the Museum was transferred to the Monastery of Monte Morcino Nuovo in 1812; in 1936, it was moved again to Palazzo Donini-Ferretti

Western arm of the cloister of St. Domenic's: an Etruscan Urn

where it remained until 1948 when it was finally settled in its present location (the former Monastery of St. Dominic). Here, it took on the status of Communal Civic Museum in 1962.

The Museum occupies part of the large Cloister and the second floor of the Monastery. In the Cloister, below the portico, Estruscan cinerary urns, inscriptions and architectural fragments are on display. Of particular interest are the following: a black and white mosaic with geometrical motifs dating back to 100 B.C. from the Perugia area; a sarcophagus showing the myth of Meleagrus (late 1000'a A.D.) from Farfa; a well-curb depicting a battle between Greeks and Amasons, also from Farfa; several Augustan memorial stones with the inscription '*Perusia restituta*'. Not far from the staircase leading up to the second floor, there is a Roman plaque with decorative motifs, used as an altar table during the Middle Ages.

Northern arm of the Cloister of St. Domenic's: well curb showing battle scenes between Greeks and Amasons

In the gallery of the second floor, numerous Etruscan urns are displayed, originating from various Perugian necropolis (400-100 B.C.), put into categories according to their place of origin. The southern section displays urns from the ten necropolis around Ponticello di Campo; the western gallery contains urns originating from the families Rafia (of Perugia), Pomponia and Plotia (the Hypogeum of the Volumni), Noforsinia (from the necropolis of the Palazzone), Titia Vetia (from San Sisto) and various others from the Monteluce area. At the centre of this gallery, there is a Perugian urn in terracotta (300 B.C.) showing the reclining figure of the deceased on the lid and the legend of the monster coming out of the well on the front. The northern gallery contains urns of various origins, including those of the following families: Trebia (from Castiglione del Lago), Tetinia (from Paciano) and Varna (from Cetona). The eastern gallery contains Roman remains, cinerary urns and inscriptions. Several inscriptions originate from Arna.

The corridor leading to the gallery of the second cloister contains several Roman portraits including a head of Claudius discovered at Carsulae; a portrait of Caesar, one of Augustua and one of a woman with a hair-style like that of Agrippina, from Carsulae and Spoleto respectively. At the end of the corridor there are two different sections: Prehistoric on the left, Etruscan/Roman on the right.

The Prehistoric section occupies eight rooms, a long corridor and a large hall; the material is displayed according to typology and the place of origin. The rooms containing works ordered according to object type (four on the right and one on the left of the corridor) display palaeolithic and neolithic material from the Bellucci Collection originating from Umbria, Tuscany, the Marches and Abruzzo. In the last three rooms, the material is arranged topographically and originates from the various prehistoric settlements existing in the region of Perugia. Leaving the corridor, a staircase leads up to the hall containing material from the Bronze and Iron Ages. Part of the Hall is occupied by material from Monte Cetona (the Calzoni excavation), dating from the

Cinerary Urn

Vase with relief work (from Cetona)

Sandstone sarcophagus (from the Sperandio area)

Bronze dagger (from Fontivegge)

Etruscan bronze statuette (from Castel St. Mariano)

middle palaeolithic age (the Gosto Grotta); and material from the Bronze age (the Carletti house).

Descending the staircase we enter the Etruscan/Roman section, at present in the process of being re-ordered. ROOM I contains a grave stele found at Monte Gualandro, originating from Tuoro, showing battle scenes (early 4th century B.C.). The corridor contains a sepulchral sphinx from the Cetona area (late 6th century).

ROOM II is host to Chiusian memorial stones with relief and polychromatic work (late 6th and 5th centuries B.C.); backing onto the far wall, is a sandstone sarcophagus from the Sperandio necropolis near Perugia, with relief-work on the front and polychromatic traces on the sides. It depicts a triumphal return from battle with banqueting scenes (late 6th century B.C.). ROOMS III and IV preserve embossed bronze laminas and statues from Castel San Marino near Corciano. The bronze laminas (some of which are on display in the British Museum) are among the rarest of the archaic bronze-work to be found in the Etruscan territories. They probably constituted the covering of a war chariot.

ROOM V contains objects from the necropolis of Monteluce whilst ROOM VI is

96

nost to material discovered in the necropolis of Frontone: of particular importance is a male funeral 'corredo' including arms, bronze kottabos and attic vase with red figures from the myth of Trittolemo and a bronze lid. ROOM VII has objects from the necropolis of Santa Caterina and Sperandio; from the first, among other interesting objects, there is a bronze situla with a siren on the lid and a gold earing (the other of which is in the British Museum). Outside ROOM VII is the famous Perugian Memorial Stone in travertine rock with one of the longest Etruscan inscriptions yet to be discovered mentioning the Velthina and Afuna families, properties and tombs. ROOM VIII accomodates material from the Perugian necropolis of Santa Giuliana, Ponticello di Campo, Monte Vile, Cimitero. ROOM IX contains objects from the sepulchres in the immediate vicinity of the city (Monte Tezio, Pila, Bettona). ROOM X displays material from Orvieto and around Castiglione del Lago: of particular interest is a Greek helmet with decorative motifs in relief and se-

Bronze situla (St. Caterina)

Etruscan bronze statuette (from Castel St. Mariano)

Perugian memorial stone

Kélebe by the Artist of Hesion

veral urns from Paciano. ROOM XI is host to votive objects from Colle Arsiccio (terracotta statues) and Caligiano di Magione as well as votive bronzes from the sanctuaries of Ancarano di Norcia and Calvi. In the corridor, we find a terracotta statue of Hercules, signed by the artist (C. Rufius s(igillator) finxit), from Compresso.

To the right of the corridor is the entrance of the 17th-century gallery in which Cypriot material (16th to 1st centuries B.C.) from the Palma di Cesnola collection is on display along with Corinthian and Etrusco-Corinthian ceramics and Attic and Etruscan ceramics with black and red figures. Without doubt, the most valuable object is the Volterran Kelebe showing the myth of Hercules and Hesion and of Hercules and Ketos attributed to the Hesion artist and dating back to around the late 4th century B.C.

Next to the Church of St. Dominic, we can take Via del Castellano which is bordered on the right by the south aisle cha-

pel walls of the church. The first three are in laterite stone and date from the 18th century. To the left of the site entrance, note the polygon-shaped rock structure of the present Chapel of the votive Madonna and, to the right, the rectangular exterior of the Chapel of St. Domenic built by Giovanni and Luchino di Pietro during the 1450's in accordance to the wishes of the Perugian merchant, Francesco di Pietro. The rhythm of the red and white stone work is interrupted by a large gothic mullioned-window; the upper region bears a dentil shaped ornamentation also in red and white stone.

Turning left, we find ourselves directly behind the apse of the church from where we can admire its external construction and large gothic windows. Opposite, we can see the **Palace of the Inquisition**, begun in 1632 and designed by Domenico

Gold earing (St. Caterina) ▶

St. Peter's Gate (Porta S. Pietro)

St. Peter's Gate: detail

Grotti. The finishing touches were added in 1710 circa. The travertine door, dated 1667, still preserves the ancient delicately wood designs.

Going back Corso Cavour, a 15th-century well-curb backs onto a building on the right.

Continuing along Corso Cavour, at no. 130, we find the former **Hospice of the Dominican Brotherhood**, originating from 1333, with an elegant black and white stone façade. Today, the building has been converted into a carpentry workshop.

Further along at no. 133, the present-day Garibaldi Barracks was the site of the **Monastery of the Blessed Colomba**; this was an estension of a pre-existing Dominican Tertiary monastery (late 15th century). A second renovation took place around 1760. On this occasion, the church (still visible within the barracks) was restored and decorated with architectural perspectives by Paolo Brizi and with various allegorical motifs by Francesco Appiani. The monastery was suppressed after the Unification of Italy. Next door, there was another religious establishment: the Benedictine convent of St. Mary Magdalen.

On the left is the Parish Church of **St. Mary of the Hill** which existed as early as 1285; it was extended during the 14th and 15th centuries and restructured in 1771 to a design by Alessio Lorenzini. It still contains an altar-piece by Benedetto Bandiera depicting Our Lady of Constantinople, St. Charled Borromeo, St. Francis and other saints (1614).

The house next to the *Auditorium Marianum* contains an early 14th-century painting of the Madonna and Child.

Porta S. Pietro (St. Peter's Gate)

Porta S. Pietro is, in fact, composed of two separate gateways. The internal one presents clear traces of successive renovations: the main part is built in ashlar-work travertine and red stone, typical of Perugian and Umbrian mediaeval constructions, and laterite. Above the arch, there is a niche containing figures of Our Lady of the Rosary between SS. Dominic and Francis; the image was painted in 1765 and re-painted in 1817. The external gateway has all the elegance of the Humanist/Renaissance period and is reminiscent of the Malatestian Temple by Alberti in Rimini. It is the work of Agostino di Antonio di Duccio and Polidoro di Stefano of Perugia and was built during the period, 1475-1480. The central arch is decorated by a festoon and the piers show evidence of the fluting of the slide gate. On either side, there are two towers with elegant parastas, surmounted by Corinthian capitals.

On the left, between the two gate-ways, we find the small travertine Renaissance portal of the **Church of St. James,** an ancient parish church (1285) which contains a painting depicting the Crucifix between SS. James and John the Baptist, signed by Benedetto Bandiera (17th century).

Continuing down Viale Benedetto Bonfigli, we can see on our left, at no. 8, the coat-of-arms of the Exchange: a griffin above a chest; this marks the site of the hospice of this guild. A little further down, on the right, we find the former *Monastery of St. Jerome.* This was the seat of the Amadean friars from 1483 to 1568, the year of their suppression by Pius V; after this, the brothers dedicated themselves to those stricken by plague; after a time, they merged with the Franciscan Observants and continued to work with them until the supression of the post Unification period. Of this monastery, we can still see an early 18th century portico designed by Pietro Carattoli and the internal cloister with its laterite archways dating from the 17th century. Further down, we find the **Alexandrian Gate** (sometimes called the **Gate of St. Jerome**). It was built towards the end of the 1400's and was recnstructed by order of the delegate Cardinal Alexander Riario in 1582.

Proceeding beyond porta S. Pietro, along Via Borgo XX Giugno, on the right, at no. 29, we come across the **Church of the Madonna di Braccio,** so called because it was erected by order of Braccio Baglioni between 1476 and 1479. It was reduced to its present form in 1782 and contains a fresco depicting the Madonna and Child which is the work of Tiberio of Assisi (16th century).

Continuing along Via Madonna di Braccio, we arrive in Viale Roma where we can see the mediaeval walls erected by Braccio Fortebracci of Montone. On the right, beyond the College of St. Anne, stands a tower with fine travertine corbels.

The present-day **College of St. Anne,** today a secondary school, was once an establishment of a female community entitled St. Mary of the Angels (Poor Clares). During the second half of the 15th century, it was taken over by the regular clergy and, around the end of the 18th century, the building was converted into an orphanage; the neo-classical façade was designed by G. Santini. Inside, we can admire the 15th-century cloister with travertine columns.

The Church of St. Peter

Proceeding along Via Borgo XX Giugno, we arrive at the **Church and Abbey of St. Peter.**

A church has existed in the area — called Monte Cavlario of Capraio — since the times of Pope Gregory the Great. In fact, tradition has it that this was the site of the first Cathedral of Perugia. The monastery is said to have been established around the year 966 A.D., on the initiative of the Blessed Pietro Vincioli, but, in reality, its origins go further back into obscurity. It is certain that, in the Roman Synod of 1002, Pope Sylvester II decided to defend the Abbot of St. Peter's against the Bishop of Perugia, Canone, who had invaded the monastery, declaring it to be the property of the Roman Church and, therefore, under the jurisdiction of the Bishop. The monastery's archive preserves a large quantity of papal privileges and imperial favours, awarded to the Abbey during the 11th and 12th centuries all evidence of its importance and wealth. Throughout the 13th century, it continued to receive papal protection and, during the reign of Gregory IX, statutes for the reform of the monastery were drawn up (1235?). During the 14th century, the monastery suffered a period of crisis and confusion; in 1398, the Perugians set fire to the monastery when they rose against Abbot Francis Guidalotti who, with his brother, was the author of the conspiracy against Biordo Michelotti, head of the popular party. In 1436, in order to relieve conditions within the monastery, Pope Eugene IV merged it with the Congregation of St. Justina of Padua. Following this union, the monastery refluorished, resuming and maintaining its prestige and power within the town. In 1799, the monastery was suppressed by the French and then restored to the monks by the provisional Austrian/Aretine Government. In reward for having assisted several leaders of the Perugian revolt of 1859, after Unification, the monks were allowed to stay on at the Abbey.

Passing through a monumental front section with three arches, designed around 1614 by the Perugian architect, Valentino Martelli, with the explicit intention of corresponding to the opposite 15th-century gateway by Agostino di Duccio, we enter into the first cloister of the monastery, the lower region of which was also designed by Valentino Martelli. The upper floor is attributed to Lorenzo Petrozzi who, after Martelli, was entrusted with the task of completing the works.

In the north cloister, we arrive at the entrance of the Church. On either side of this Quattrocento doorway, surmounted by a lunette and attributed to Giannicola di Paolo, we can see the remains of the ancient façade of the basilica which included a portico of small arches in red and white and 13th and 14th-century frescoes. Right of the doorway, the base of the large polygon shaped bell-towers is still visible: we can still recognise the gothic forms of the Tuscan type which originated from the 15th-century reconstruction, particularly in the bell-tower and spire, attributed to the Florentine, Giovanni di Betto and Pietro di Firenze, working to a design by Bernardo Rossellino (1463-1468).

Its interior with a nave and two aisles, contains the finest art collection in Perugia after the Umbrian National Gallery.

The nave is divided from the aisles by a series of arches, sustained by columns probably originating from ancient Roman buildings. The upper regions are decorated with large canvases depicting scenes from the New and Old Testaments paired with panels according to the theological and didactic contents which are clearly linked to Counter-Reformation doctrine. This scheme presents a unified iconographical programme, including the pictures in the presbytery, which was almost cer-

The Church of St. Peter

tainly the idea of Abbot Don Giacomo da San Felice of Salò and it was arranged between 1591 and 1611. The canvases are the work of Antonio Vassillacchi, alias the 'Alinese', a disciple of Veronese but, above all, of Tintoretto, and were painted in Venice between 1593 and 1594.

Beginning from the right, they are as follows: the Birth of Jesus and Isaac blessing Jacob; the Dispute with the Doctors and the Queen of Sheba admiring the wisdom of Solomon; the Baptism of Christ and Naaman cured of Leprosy; the Wedding of Cana and the meal given by Abraham to the three angels; Jesus dining with the Pharisee and the penitence of David when reproved by the Prophet Natham; the Resurrection of Lazarus and Elias raising from the dead, the son of the widow of Sereptas; the Expulsion of the Merchants from the Temple and Moses breaking the tablets of the cammandments; the Entrance of Jesus into Jerusalem and David conquering Goliath, the Crucifixion and the Sacrifice of Isaac; the Resurrection and Jonah surrended by the Whale.

The large canvas depicting the Triumph

Bell tower (15th century)

Historic façade

Interior

of the Benedicting Order, on the inner-façade wall, is also by Antonio Vassillacchi.

The frescoes on the walls are attributed to Giovanni Maria Bisconti whilst the ovals, set within the triangles of the arches showing the busts of various Popes, are the work of Benedetto Bandiera who also painted the Virgin and the Archangel Gabriel on the triumphal arch. The decorations on the vault of the south aisle are probably by Scilla Pecennini and Benedetto Bandiera; whilst those in the north aisle, unfortunately much re-painted, bear a marked resemblance to the work of Mattia Salvucci of Perugia.

On either side of the outer door, made by Pompeo Dardoni in 1682, there are detached frescoes by Orazio Alfani and Leonardo Cungi from Borgo San Sepolcro (1556). The former painted the ones on the left depicting St. Peter healing the Cripple and St. Peter being freed from the prison; Cungi painted the Shipwreck of St. Paul and St. Paul landing in Malta.

The ceiling of the nave, with carved and gold-plated box vaulting, is the work of Benedetto di Giovanni Pierantonio of Montepulciano (1564).

Beginning our tour of the church from the south aisle, the first work we meet is a Virgin and Child between SS. Mary Magdalen and George by Eusebio da San Giorgio (16th century). There follows a panel depicting the Assumption of Mary with the Apostles, by Orazio Alfani (16th century). The canvas above the following altar showing St. Scolastica is by Francesco Appiani (1751). Further on, we find a canvas by the Classical artist, Giacinto Gimignani with St. Peter stopping a falling column with a sign of the cross (1679). The second altar has a canvas by Cesare Sermei of Assisi depicting St. Marius resurrecting a man from the dead. The following painting of David choosing among the three punishments threatened by the angel, is by the Sienese baroque artist, Ventura Salimbeni (1602). The hanging canvas above the third altar shows the Procession of Penitence made in Rome by St. Gregory the Great together with the people at the time of the Great Plague. It also includes a panel attributed to Eusebio da San Giorgio who was author of the predella depicting scenes from the life of St. Christine (16th century). A little futher ahead, we arrive at the chapel of St. Joseph, commissioned in 1855 by the Abbot, Placido Acquacotta. It was painted by the Perugian artist Domenico Bruschi, assisted by Giovanni Panti. The altar painting which was recently stolen was a copy of a Raphael by Carlo Fantacchiotti (19th century). The entrance is surmounted by a lunette in the Perugian style depicting Our Lady, the Holy Child and four Saints (16th century); the panel on the right-hand wall of the Virgin and Child and SS. John and Elizabeth (16th century) is of the Tuscan school. Going back into the nave, we immediately come across a painting by the French artist, Francios Perrier depicting Samson destroying the columns of the temple (17th century). Opposite, there is a fine Pietà of the school of Sebastiano del Piombo (16th century). Following this, is the door leading into the monastery, above which are three square panels: the central one, of the Venetian school resembles the style of Bonifacio da Verona; the lateral ones, depicting St. Placido and St. Marius are copied from Perugino by Giovan Battista Salvi, alias 'Sassoferrato' (17th century).

Opposite, is a Virgin and Child by the Perugian classicist, Giovan Domenico Cerrini (17th century). This artist also painted the St. John the Baptist above the gap leading into the Presbystery area. Just before the Sacristy door, there is a Resurrection of Christ by Orazio Alfani (1553).

Above the door, there are three square panels depicting St. Flavia, St. Apollonia and St. Catherine of Sassoferrato (the last two of which are copies of works by Perugino). The far end of the aisle is host to the Chapel of the Relics or of the Angels with a 16th-century wrought-iron grille, late 16th-century stucco work and rather damaged frescoes by Benedetto Bandiera (1602 circa). This artist also painted the altar-piece depicting St. Benedict in Glory among the angels, at present to be seen in the Great Hall of the Faculty of Agriculture.

The Sacristy (1451) has a vault bearing frescoes with stories from the Old Testament framed by decorative motifs tradionally attributed to the Perugian artist, Scilla Pecennini. However, it is more probable that they are the work of an artist connected with the Nordic and Flemish presence documented in Perugia during the 1560's. The wall frescoes depicting the lives of SS. Peter and Paul are by Girolamo Danti (1574), an artist of Varsarian formation. The majolica floor, traces of which are visible in front of the altar, is a splendid work by Giacomo Mantini (El frate) and dates back to 1563-64. The wardrobes were made by Giusto di Francesco di Incisa and Giovanni di Filippo da Fiesole (1472). On the altar, by Guido di Virio of Settignano and also decorated with paintings by Girolamo Danti, there is a bronze Crucifix by Algardi (17th century). There are numerous small paintings on the wall including a series of Saints by Perugino (St. Costanzo, St. Peter Abbot, St. Herculanus and St. Scolastica - a copy of the original) which together with others belong to the altar-piece of the Ascension today in the Museum of Lyon (1496); a panel with two cherubs by an imitator of Perugino, inspired by the Holy Family in the Museum of Marseille; two canvases in the style of Caravaggio (St. Frances Romana and Christ with the Crown of Thorns); a head of Christ resembling the style of Dosso Dossi; a 16th-century Holy Family of the Emilian school and a Visitatio by a disciple of Sebastiano Conca.

Going back into the aisle, we find ourselves in the area of the Presbytery. The two polygon-shaped stone pulpits are the work of Francesco da Guido of Settignano, made between 1487 and 1530; the seat has a wealth of gold-plated carvings by Benedetto da Montepulciano and Benvenuto da Brescia (1555-56). Of the two organs, the one nearer the Sacristy was almost completely remade in 1591. The lower part is decorated with allegorical figures attributed to Benedetto Bandiera but was carried out with the help of an unknown baroque artist of great stylistic elegance. The other organ is the work of a certain Maestro Dionigi (1615).

The main altar was originally decorated with paintings by Giannicola di Paolo and with Perugino's famous Ascension, now in the Museum of Lyon; it was completely remade by Valentino Martelli between

1592 and 1608. Martelli also designed the ciborium, made in Rome by Ghetti between 1627 and 1635. The large canopy above the altar is the work of Benedetto Bandiera who also painted the Four Evangelists on the vault (1591) and the canvas in the apse depicting the Death of St. Benedict. The inner front of the triumphal arch is decorated with harvesting and reaping scenes taken from the Apocalypse and attributed to Giovanni Fiammingo of Anvers (1592). The vault between the presbytery and chior (God the Father among the Angels) and the lunettes between the ribbing of the apse (The Theological and Cardinal Virtues) are painted by Scilla Pecennini with the collaboration of Pietro d'Alessandro (1594). Finally, we come across the two famous scenes of the Consignment of the Keys to St. Peter and the Conversion of St. Paul, attached to the walls above the choir, painted by Gio-

Wooden choir and frescoes in the apse (16th century)

van Battista Lombardelli della Maria in 1591.

The choir is certainly one of the most beautiful to be found in Italy. It was begun in 1525-26 by Bernardino di Luca Antonibi of Perugia with the collaboration of Niccolò di Stefano of Bologna. After a long interruption, probably owing to the plague, the work was resumed in 1533 by Stefano di Antoniolo Zambelli of Bergamo and his assistants (Grisello, Tommaso, Nicola and Antonio from Florence; the Bolognese artist, Battista; the Frenchman, Ambrogio; the Dalmatian, Domenico Schiavone and Niccolò di Antonio di Ludovico from Cagli). The work was finished in 1535. The signature of Stefano da Bergano is visible at the head of the cymatium. The beautiful door of the choir depicts the Annunciation and Moses saved from the Red Sea and was made by Frà Damiano of Bergamo brother of Stefano, in 1536 (his signature and the date are visible beneath the railing). The large lectern in the choir was made in 1536-37 by two of Stefano's assistants: Battista from Bologna and Ambrogio from France. From the inlaid door, we pass onto a small terrace affording a splendid view of the Assisi valley.

Entering the north aisle, on the far wall, there is a Pietà between SS. Jerome and Leonard, dated 1469 and thought to be an early work of Fiorenzo di Lorenzo (though some believe it to be the work of Benedetto Bonfigli or Nicolò del Prione). Below it, we find the tombstone of Bishop Ugolino da Montevibiano (+ 1319). A painting depicting Christ in the Garden, attributed to Giovanni Lanfranco (17th century) hangs in the left-hand corner. There follows the entrance of the Vibi Chapel, built in 1473 and renovated in 1506 by Francesco di Guido of Settignano. The work was financed by Baglione Vibi, a nobleman from Montevibio. The splendid marble altar-frontal showing the Child Jesus, the Baptist and St. Jerome is agreed to be the work of Mino da Fiesole (1473, see inscription). Within the lunette above this, there is an Annunciation by Giovan Battista Caporali (1521) who is also author of the remaining decorative fragments on the walls and vault. To the left is a painting of the Visitation by Polidoro di Stefano Ciburri of Perugia (1530); to the right, we see a copy of Giovanni Spagna's Madonna of the Lily by Sassoferrato.

Returning into the aisle, we find ourselves directly in front of a painting of St. Paul the Apostle after the style of Guercino; a little further ahead, on the opposite wall, there is a painting of Christ laid in the Tomb, copied from Baglioni di Raffaello's Deposition by Sassoferrato (the original is in the Borghese Gallery in Rome). The next chapel, which first be-

Wooden choir: detail (16th century)

longed to the Baglioni family and then to the Ranieri family, was also built to a plan by Francesco di Guido of Settignano (1505). The vault, originally decorated with frescoes by Giovan Battista Caporali, now bears paintings by Annibale Brugnoli (1863); on the left-hand wall, we see a painting of Jesus in the Garden by Guido Reni; on the right, there is a canvas depicting Jesus with Veronica by the Bolognese artist, Giovan Francesco Gessi (17th century). Opposite the chapel there is a painting of St. Paul. On the walls in front of this, we find a canvas by Sassoferrato (17th century) depicting Judith with the head of Holofernes.

Next is the Chapel of the Sacrament with a vault decorated by Francesco Appiani with perspective square panels by Pietro Carattoli (1762-63); above the altar hangs an ancient image of the Madonna of the Lily of the Perugian school; this work dates back to the early 1500's and was taken from the Valiano villa in 1643; on either side, there are paintings (SS. Peter and Paul) by Giovan Battista Wicar (19th century). The right-hand wall bears

Mino da Fiesole (?): gold-plated marble altar-frontal (15th century)

Fiorenzo di Lorenzo (?): Pietà (15th century) and details of Saint Geronimo and Saint Leonard

**Giovan Battista Salvi (Sassoferrato): Judith
with the head of Holophernes (17th century)**

a large canvas by Giorgio Vasari (1566)
showing the Prophet Elijah and St. Benedict. The left-hand wall has a painting of
St. Benedict sending St. Marius to France
by Giovanni Fiammingo (16th century)
and the Wedding of Cana by Vasari.

Back in the aisle, on the following column, there is an Adoration of the Magi
by Eusebio da San Giorgio (1508). A
staircase leads down into excavations recently carried out which reveal the foundations of a pre-existing structure dating
back to the High Mediaeval period.

The next altar we come to has an Assumption of Our Lady by Orazio Alfani
(16th century). Further on, we come to an
Annunciation by Sassoferrato and an altar with a wooden Crucifix, dating 1478
and attributed the Eusebio Bastoni of Pe-

rugia. A little further ahead, the panel
showing the Pietà is a late work by Perugino and originates from the Church of
St. Augustine. The next altar has a painting of St. Peter Uincioli by Appiani
(1751). At the end of aisle, the paintings
of St. Marius and St. Placido are by Giacinto Giminiani (1677).

Next to the canvases by Giminiani, we
find a door leading into a room containing many precious illustrated books (hy-
mnals, catechisms, graduals and antiphonaries) originating from the 15th and 16th
centuries.

Returning into the first cloister through
a corridor on the left, which reveals the
impressive foundations of the bell-tower,
we enter the second, Renaissance-style,
main cloister attributed to Francesco di
Guido of Settignano (16th century); it has
a well in the centre by Galeotto di Paolo
of Assisi (1530). Under the portico on the
west side, we can still see the door and
two mullioned windows of the former
Charter House. Further on, we come to
the entrance of the ancient refectory, the
atrium of which contains a fine lavabo
with a large stained-glass lunette showing
the Woman of Samaria at the well; it is attributed to the Florentine artist, Benedetto de Zuanni, alias 'Buglione' (1487-88).
Passing through another corridor, we
leave the main cloister and enter the 'new'
cloister (also called the Cloister of the
Stars) which was designed by Alessi in
1571.

Today, the monastery is the seat of the
Foundation of Agricultural Education,
formed in 1887, and the Faculty of Agriculture of the University of Perugia.

In front of the Abbey is the fine **Frontone Garden**; Braccio Fortebracci, governor of Perugia from 1416 to 1424, used
this space as a weapon store; from 1569
on, it became the location of the live-
stock market which took place during the
All Saints' Day Fair. At the beginning of
the 1700's, the site was donated to the Ar-
cadians; this marked the beginning of its
transformation into a pleasant garden;
between 1778-80, the amphitheatre was
built, at the centre of which is an arch designed by Baldassarre Orsini, erected in
1791.

One leaves the monastery grounds via
porta di St. Costanzo which was designed
by Valentino Martelli and built in 1586-

110

Eusebio da S. Giorgio: The Adoration of the Magi (16th century) and a detail.

87. It comprises laterite columns above which is the coat-of-arms of the Abbey of St. Peter. This is surmounted by a large cornice and an attic which contains the coat-of-arms of Sextus V in travertine stone. (The mediaeval porta of St. Costanzo is situated in the Botanical Gardens of the Faculty of Agriculture).

Going down the steps opposite the porta, we come to the **Church of St. Costanzo**, named after the traditional figure of the Bishop of Perugia, who was martyred during the reign of Emperor Marcus Aurelius. The church already existed as early as 1027. It has always belonged to the nearby Abbey of St. Peter. In 1205, after a renovation, the church was consecrated, as is proved by the inscription on the main altar under which the relics of the mar-

Miniatured coral (15th century)

tyred Bishop were said to have been found in 1781. In the 1890's, the church was completely rebuilt in the neo-Romantic style by the Perugian architect, Guglielmo Calderini. Of the mediaeval edifice, there remains the outer wall of the apse; its portal is a fine example of Romanic sculpture (late 12th century) and is composed of two marble jambs decorated with leafy patterns and fantastic animals; on the architrave is the figure of Christ surmounted by the symbols of the Four Evangelists.

On the return journey along Corso Cavour, we can turn into Via Podiani in which the Palazzo Della Penna is situated, soon to become the home of the **Museum of Modern and Contemporary Art**. This building was reconstructed, along with the nearby Palazzo Rossi Scotti, during the first two decades of the 1800's; the remains of a Roman amphitheatre have been found in this area. From here, we ascend the steps of Via Vibi and arrive at the **Porta dei Funari**, built in calcareous rock up to the trusses; the upper part is in laterite and is supported by travertine trusses.

The Main Cloister   **Palazzo Della Penna ▶**

The Rocca Paolina

From Via Podiani, we enter Viale Indipendenza. A short way ahead, turning immediately to the right into Via Marzia, we can walk alongside the last remaing spur buttress of the **Rocca Paolina**.

It is documented that the Rocca Paolina was a concrete political and military symbol of authority over the «riotous city». In fact, this fortress was built by Paolo III after the salt war in order to keep the city under control once and for all. It was built to a design by Antonio and Aristotile da Sangallo in record time (1530-1543). A quarter of the city was demolished in order to construct it (the houses of the Baglioni family, the St. Giuliana quarter, the Church of St. Mary of the Servants and many others). Sangallo managed to save the Etruscan **Porta Marzia** by integrating in into the wall structure, leaving it still visible above the doorway. The porta is a composed of an arch underlined by a row of hewn rocks and a slightly protruding cornice. A horizontal strip, bearing the inscription *Augusta Perusia* acts as a base to a gallery comprising Italo-Conrinthian pillars between which five figures are placed. This ensemble is symmetrically arranged between two Italo-Corinthian columns, parting from the base of the arch which, together with the other smaller columns, support the upper protruding cornice bearing the inscription *Colonia Vibia*. The three figures in the gallery have been identified as Gastor, Jove and Polluce. On the sides, there are two figures of horses. The jambs of the door are visible, in their original position, at the entrance of the Rocca. Inside, we recognise traces of ancient roads (Via Bagliona etc.), piazzas, buildings and towers which were incorporated into the foundations of the fortress. It was an impressive edifice based around a wast central nucleus, linked by a long corridor (120 metres approximately) to the sentry areas towards the city's edge. Within this central complex, there stood the Captain's Palace, designed by Galeazzo Alessi, and adorned by a beautiful loggia, also designed by Alessi (although some believe it to be the work of Raffaello da Montelupo); the rooms of the building had frescoes by various artists: Cristoforo

The Rocca Paolina and Porta Marzia

The Church of the Holy Spirit: Interior (17th century)

rely in travertine rock; above, several travertine corbels support small arches and a wall face in laterite.

The Church of S. Spirito (the Holy Spirit)

Beyond the porta, on the left, we turn into Via del Parione; after a short stretch of road, we find ourselves in front of the **Church of S. Spirito**. This was the seat of a Benedictine female community, listed among the Perugian dependencies of the Abbey of Farneta, in a document drawn up by Henry II in 1014, although several doubts exist as the validity of this document. However, the convent certainly esisted in the 13th century. In the early 15th century, after a series of mergers had taken place, the convent ceased to exist. The site was given to the Minimi family in 1576, and the construction of a new church commenced in 1578 following a design by Giovanni Francesco Vezzosi of

Pistoia. It was completed in 1689 and consacrated in 1691. At present, it functions as a parish church. The classical interior has a wall divided into three separate sections, each of which has an arch acting as a niche for an altar; the curved gallery is scanned by five blind arches.

The first two altars, right and left of the nave, contain false architectural perspectives by Pietro Carattoli (18th century). The first altar on the right is host to a Madonna and Child with St. Michael the Archangel by Francesco Busti (18th century). The following altar shows the Trinity contemplated by SS. Gaspar of Valenza, Leonardo de' Longobardis and Francis Salesio, by Cristoforo Gasperi (1788). The third altar, in carved gold-plated wood dating back to the late 1600's, has a central niche contining an image of St. Francis of Paolo (17th century). The large canvas at the centre of the apse, depicting the Descent of the Holy Spirit, is the work of Lazzaro Baldi. The canvas on the right shows St. Peter giving Baptisms and the one on the right shows St. Peter giving Confirmations; both works originate from the Baldi school (17th century). The pews, made out of walnut in the Choir, date from the 18th century. The inner-façade wall bears two canvases attributed to Mattia Batini (18th century). From here, the left-hand wall of the nave has an altar which is host to a canvas by Giacinto Boccanera (1731) depicting St. Spiridione administering the Sacrament of Baptism to Emperor Costante. The second altar (the altar of the goldsmiths) has a canvas by Mattia Battini (18th century) depicting Andronicus and Atanasia expressing resignation for the loss of their children. The third altar comprises a relief in carved multicoloured wood with decorative stucco-work (18th century).

Returning along Via del Parione, we turn into Via S. Giacomo. At no. 50, we notice the travertine Renaissance portal of the former **Parish Church of St. Giacomo** of porta Eburnea (1285 circa), now used as a warehouse. Going ahead, we take Via delle Forze at the end of which we come across the mediaeval porta S. Giacomo (of St. James); if, on the other hand, we prefer to go down Via Eburnia, we come to the 16th-century **porta Eburnea** (1576) built by order of Governor Santacroce (for this reason, sometimes referred to as porta Crucia), and attributed to Valentino Martelli. Here, as elsewhere, we recognise a case of a mediaeval borgo which developed outside the city walls creating the necessity of new walls and new city gates; thus, both the ancient porta Eburnea and the mediaeval porta of St. Giacomo are clearly visible.

The Church of St. Prosperus

Coming out of Via Eburnea and turning right, we cover a short stretch of Viale Pompeo Pellini and then turn left into Via S. Prospero in order to visit the church of the same name.

It is commonly thought that the foundations of the **Church of St. Prosperus** dated back to the 7th or 8th centuries; it was certainly a religious and cultural centre during the early 13th century when Bonamico worked there; in 1285, it was listed among the parish churches of the porta Eburnea area; in 1302, we find it in the Cathedral Charter to which it belonged until the end of the 16th century although, in 1436, it was included among the properties of the Abbey of Pomposa. In 1609, it became a seminary; during the 18th century it was taken over by the Missionary Fathers and finally by the Donini family; after this, the church traversed a period of neglect and decline up to around 1920, then it was re-opened by the original order when important frescoes were discovered by Ettore Ricci (1927).

It is an aisleless church with a barrel vault and was perhaps originally covered by a tie-beam. It contains a ciborium dating back to the mid-9th century with decorative motifs inspired by the paleo-Christian ethos and probably prompted by the cultural influence of Ravenna (rosettes, fan-tails, reversed mirrors = the rejection of vanity etc.). However, there are also classical elements such as intertwining leafy patterns. Behind the ciborium, is a statue of St. Prosperus dating back to the 18th century. On the right-hand wall, an archway leads into the only chapel, with the vault and walls bearing frescoes signed by Bonamico and dated 1225 (see inscription). The vault is divided into two areas by a decorative strip of leafy motifs. The twelve Apostles are arranged in a line above the entrance; on the other side, the following prophets are depicted-Osea, Joel, Sofonias, Daniel, Abdias, Jonas and Micheas. The lunettes on the two shorter walls had frescoes of the Annunciation (on the right) of which only a fragment showing the angel is left, and the Birth of Jesus (on the left) which has now completely disappeared, but which was still visible at the beginning of the century. Beneath the fresco depicting the Annunciation, we see John the Baptist with St. Herculanus at his side; beneath the Nativity Scene, there are traces of a fresco depicting St. Paul, St. Lucy and the Virgins Lucy and Catherine. The far wall has a fresco showing (from left to right) Mary Magdelen, St. Margaret, St. Brigit, St. Illuminata, St. Michael the Ar-

The Church of St. Prosperus: High Mediaeval ciborium (7th - 8th century) ▶

changel, Abraham and the Angel of the Shadows (?). On the same wall, there used to be a second strip of frescoes terminating at ground level; today, slight traces of St. Leonard, St. Benedict, St. Nicholas of Bari and St. Sylvestre are still visible. The strip was surrounded by fake drapery of which only a few fragments remains. On the wall of the entrance, a group of nuns and an image of Giovanni da Perugia are visible.

The Church of St. Juliana

(S. Giuliana)

Returning from St. Prosperus, we take Viale Pellini, Via Fiorenzo di Lorenzo and then turn right into Viale Baldassarre Orsini. A short distance ahead, we reach the **Church and former Convent of St. Juliana**.

Although precise information regarding its pre-history is lacking, the official date of the foundation of the convent was 1253, when a group of papal letters and a solemn favour were sent to the Perugian convent by Pope Innocence IV, declaring it to be under the protection of the Holy See, affirming the rules of the Benedictine Order according to the Cistercian statue, conceding it ecclesiastical privileges and confirming its ownership of its acquired properties. It was the Cistercian Cardinal, Giovanni da Toledo, who promoted the consolidation of this new and powerful female monastic movement when, in the same year (1253), he assigned the convent to the jurisdiction of the Abbot of St. Galgano (Diocese of Volterra), an act which was confirmed by the Abbot of Citeaux in 1260. The origins of the Cistercian convent are to be found outside the city, though nearby, between porta S. Pietro and Porta Eburnea. It is almost as if its development was intended to counterbalance that of the Poor Clares at Monteluce (cf. further on). Thanks to the support of the city's most important families, the convent became one of the richest and most prestigious in Perugia. From the 14th century on, the convent entered a phase of moral decline and decadence which culminated in the early-16th century, by which time the nuns completely ignored the rules of community life within the cloister. The ill fame of the mo-nastery, which probably provided the background for Agnolo Firenzuola's most risqué short story, reached the ears of the popes and Paul III attempted a reform of the convent. In 1567, Pius V placed it under the direct jurisdicion of the Bishop of Perugia, definitively severing it from the Cistercians. All subsequent bishops were diligent in the reform of the convent throughout the late-16th century; its religious and moral welfare appears to have improved during the 17th century. With the Napoleonic suppression, the Church was used as a granary; after the Unification, it became (and still is) a military hospital. The church was reopened in 1937.

The double skewed façade, covered in red stone squares bordered by strips of white, has a portal with a rounded arch decorated with a trilobe and capitals bearing finely carved acanthus leaves. There is an identical doorway on the north flank of the Church. Above is an elegant rose-window.

Its aisleless, tie-beamed interior reveals numerous traces of its ancient pictorical decoration. From the surviving fragments we deduce that the far wall was host to a large composition. On the walls of the nave, traces are still visible of an upper decorative strip more or less at the level of the windows. Another strip, about four metres in width, began at ground level and ran along all the walls of the building. The triumphal arch, major sections of which still remain, was decorated both externally and internally. The exterior surface of the piers still bears 'larger than life' figures: on the right, St. Juliana; on the left, St. Bernard of Chiaravalle holding the crosier and rules of the order. The front of the arch is decorated with ornamental motifs of alternated large and small circles. The smaller circles contain fake marble incrustations, the large ones contain images of the Four Evangelists, the mystic angel and twelve figures of angels. This allusion to the triumph of the Church has a symbolic relationship to the images of the saints (emblem of the militancy of the Church) which were originally arranged along the walls of the nave;

The Church and Garden of St. Juliana ▶

122

today, we can see traces of St. Pier Damiani and Pope Gregory VII on the right-hand wall. The upper wall of the apse bears a large fresco depicting the Coronation of Our Lady which, together with the one depicting the Last Supper on the left-hand wall of the nave, comes from the refectory of the convent. Recently, critics have tended to attribute these frescoes to the author of triptych no. 14 in the Umbrian National Gallery (mid-13th century). We find other mid-13th century frescoes (unfortunately much demaged) in the ancient Chapter Room which leads into the convent's large cloister. We reach the cloister via a passage-way which reveals traces of the previous 13th-century one in the French gothic style. The present cloister is a splendid example of 14th-century Cistercian architecture and is attributed to Matteo Gattapone. The style of the upper section with its three lighted mullioned windows, leads us to suppose that a later intervention took place, carried out by masters of the Lombard school. The second capital in the corner near the entrance (perhaps originating from the previous cloister) reveals a Romanic figurative style: it has images of St. Herculanus, a French king holding a lily (perhaps St. Louis, who took part in the se-

cond crusade prompted by the preachings of St. Bernard), a doctor of the church holding the lily of France and the Rule of the order (St. Bernard?) and St. Michael the Archangel. The third capital also has decorative reliefs showing the martyrdom of St. Juliana. From the cloister we can see the church's high bell-tower and spire, the foundations of which date back to the 13th century; the upper section is thought to have been built at the same time as the cloister (ie. 14th century). The well in the centre of the cloister is dated 1466. There are more interesting traces of frescoes to be seen in a room at the base of the bell-tower and in an attic adjacent to the pharmacy; the latter is thought to have been the room of the Abbess and has fake brocade relief work on the walls with lively decorative motifs and a niche containing a 14th-century Crucifix.

From the steps of the Church of St. Juliana, after a brief stretch of Via XX Settembre, we descend towards the station along Via del Cavallaccio. At the end of this street, we come to the Veggio Fountain, the construction of which was ordered by Paul V, under the auspices of Cardinal Scipione Borghese (between 1615 and 1624), supervised by the Perugian sculptor, Matteuccio Salvucci.

If we prefer not to descend via the Porta della Mandorla, we can take an alternative route, following Via Annibale Mariotti. At no. 2, there is a fine 15th-century cloister with secular frescoes. Further ahead, we find ourselves in Piazza Mariotti. The convent of the Poor Nuns (or of Monna Simona) stood in this square, governed by the rule of the Servants of Mary; this community grew up during the 15th century and expanded after the suppression of the parish church of St. Bartholomew (1615), during the early 17th century. Today, the area occupied by the convent is used for private apartments and secular activities. Overlooking the piazza, is the **Church of the Brotherhood of the 'Annunziata'** (first documented in 1334) which had its seat between the convent of the Poor Nuns and the Parish Church of St. Bartholomew; after the suppression of the latter, the convent took over the monks previous establish-

Capital of the Cloister (13th century)

Cloister and bell-tower ▶

ment, whilst the Brotherhood occupied the former parish church. Today, it contains frescoes by Domenico Bruschi (1900-1901).

Passing under an archway, we arrive in Via della Cupa. From here, we can admire one of the best preserved stretches of the ancient Etruscan city wall. The Commune was always very diligent in its protection and renovation of this area of Perugia. Evidence of mediaeval restoration in clearly visible in the presence of younger travertine, calcareous rock and sandstone. On the left flank we see the results of the numerous attempts at reinforcement of the more precipitous sections.

At no. 5, we find the **College della Sapenza Vecchia** (now used as a boarding school for orphans). It was founded by Cardinal Nicolò Capocci in 1361 to accomodate young men who had been reccomended by bishops from all over Europe, so that they could study at the Perugian *Studium* free of charge. The building was completed in 1369. The travertine portal we see today is in the Renaissance style. The main courtyard contains a cistern surmounted by a twelve-sided well curb with small columns at each corner. This is thought to have been built at the same time as the college but the six columns supporting the architrave and hexagonal cornice were added at the end of the 16th century. The chapel contains a fragmented late-16th century Crucifixion.

Next door to the College della Sapienza, is the ancient **Church of St. Mary of the Valley**, listed among the dependencies of the Abbey of Farneta in an uncertain document supposedly issued by Henry II in 1014. If this document is false, it is still certain that the church depended on Farneto, as affirmed in a favour issues by Pope Adrian IV in 1155 and by Clement III in 1188. It was the ancient seat of hermit monks and perhaps of the Carmelite brothers. From 1285 to 1733, it was a parish church. In 1760, it passed into the hands of the Builders' Guild — named after St. Marino — founded in 1578 and having

has several different seats prior to this; the church was restored in 1771. Towards the end of the 19th century the guild dispersed. Today, the church and its annexes belong to the Oblate Sisters of St. Francis of Sale. The interior of the church is neoclassical in style and contains a large canvas depicting the Assumption of the Virgin between SS. Lawrence and Charles Borromeo by Simeone Ciburri (1612 circa). There is also an 18th-century painting of St. Francis of Sales, a pietà dating back to the 17th century and an 18th-century painting of St. Marino. Taking Via della Luna and turning left, we see the apse of the mediaeval church.

Continuing along Via della Cupa, we turn left to find the entrance to the Cupa Gardens which follow the course of the Etruscan wall. A short distance ahead, we come to Piazza del Drago; passing beneath an archway, we arrive in a small square from which we can see the walls of the Cupa; to the right, we see the imposing edifice — with protrunding apse — of St. Benedict's. Its exact historical background is unknown except for the fact that it belonged to the Knights of Malta at least from the end of the 13th century. During the late-18th century, the Benincasa Conservatory was founded in this area, enlarged between 1777 and 1784, to accomodate and instruct young girls from the age of twelve until finding them a definitive employment.

From Piazza del Drago we take Via Benincasa and turn into Via Deliziosa where, at no. 10, we find the mediaeval double-skewed façade and bell-tower of the former parish **Church of St. Antony**, listed among the dependencies of the Cathedral Charter as early as 1163; this parish merged with that of the **Church of Santa Croce** — situated further along Via Benincasa — in 1802; at no. 17, we find a plaque recording the fact that the famous artist, Perugino, lived here.

At the end of Via Deliziosa, we go back into Via della Cupa; turning left, we return into Via dei Priori.

ITINERARY VI

The Church of the Company of Death (Compagnia della Morte)

Piazza Piccinino is bordered by the 17th-century Palazzo Sorbello. Inside, we find an Etruscan well and **Church of the Company of Death**. The Company was founded in 1570 with the aim of providing a decent burial for poor Christians found dead in the streets of the town; although devoid of its original meaning, the company still exists. The construction of the building was begun in 1575, both supervised as well as designed by Bino Sozi of Perugia; works went on until their completion at the beginning of the 1600. The church has the shape of a Greek Cross with a cupola placed above a high tiburio; the elegant Mannerist doorway was completed in 1606. The interior was renovated during the 18th century and has numerous stucco-work decorations and interesting paintings. Beginning from the right arm of the Cross, the first canvas on the right depicts St. Antony and the Virgin and Child — a work by Francesco Busti (18th century); the painting of St. Peter of Alcantara and the one depicting St. Francis Saverio are by the same author. The painting showing St. Francis of Sales — on the left-hand wall — is thought to originate from the Conca school (18th century). Above the altar is an 18th-century canvas depicting Our Lady of Mercy. The north arm has a 17th-century wooden Crucifix above the altar. It also contains (from left to right) a painting of the Madonna and Child and St. Philip Neri by Francesco Busti; a St. Francis of Assisi with an angel by Cristoforo Gasperi (18th century); St. Giacinto preaching the devotion to the Rosary, also by Gasperi; and a St. Francis of Paola originating from the Conca school, above the main altar, framed by a beautiful sculpted and gold-plated 17th-century cornice, there is a canvas by Vincenzo Pellegrini — known as the 'Pittor Bello' — depicting All Saints' Day (1612). To the left, is the Annunciation with the Eternal Father by an anonimous 18th-century artist; opposite, we see a painting of St. Antony Abbot and St. Paul the Hermit by Giacomo Mignani (18th centu-

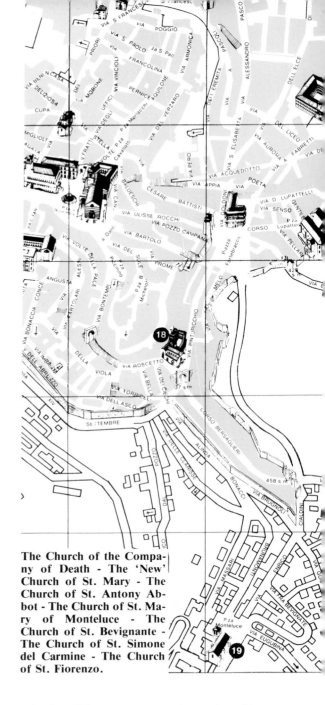

The Church of the Company of Death - The 'New' Church of St. Mary - The Church of St. Antony Abbot - The Church of St. Mary of Monteluce - The Church of St. Bevignante - The Church of St. Simone del Carmine - The Church of St. Fiorenzo.

ry); the 18th-century Perugian arist, Anton Maria Garbi painted the canvases depicting St. Joseph with the Child Jesus and St. Gregory Taumaturgo which hang on either side of the main altar. In the Sacristy (begun in 1613) we find some 17th-century walnut pews; its altar, with false architectural perspectives by Pietro Ca-

127

The Church of the Company of Death: Vincenzo Pellegrini, All Saints (17th century)

rattoli, is host to a 17th century canvas depicting St. Charles Borromeo.

Continuing along Via Bontempi with its noble palazzi, we come to no. 21, where remains (a calcareous rock wall with a single light window) of the ancient **Church fo St. Mary Magdalen** are visible. This was once the oratory of the Friars of Penitence (Franciscan tertiaries) of Perugia; the city's Bishop granted them permission the celebrate the sacred right in 1285. In the early 1400's, it passed into the hands of the Olivetans of Monte Morcino; in 1796, the church was disconsecrated and converted to secular use.

A little further ahead, is the porta dei Gigli (Gate of the Lilies), one of the best preserved gates of the Etruscan wall. The rows of large slabs reach a considerable height and it is probable that the façade of the arch was enforced by two concentric series of stone strips.

The 'New' Church of St. Mary

Descending a series of steps, we turn into Via del Roscetto, at the end of which, on the left, is situated the **New Church of St. Mary** (S. Maria Nuova). Without doubt, this was a parish church in 1285, although it had probably been one for quite some time previous to this. It passed into the hands of the Sylvestrines between the end of the 13th century and the beginning of the 14th century; it remained with the monks until the construction of the Rocca Paolina which brought about the destruction of the Church of St. Mary of the Servants; at this point, S. Maria Nuova was taken over by the 'Serviti' (the Servants), whilst the Sylvestrine monks moved to the nearby Church of St. Fortunato.

The flank of the building is made up of a mediaeval wall with a portal and two ogival arches. The façade with its simple travertine doorway, is preceded by a double-flighted staircase and a fountain which was built in 1568 and restored in 1722.

The interior has a nave a two aisles and has vaulting which dates from the 16th century although it was restored during

The Gate of the Lilies (Porta Gigli)

the 19th century. Traces of the old gothic structure are still visible in the apse and in the chapels of the minor aisles. The inner-façade wall is almost entirely occupied by the huge organ which was designed by Bino Sozi, carved by Marco Pace and decorated by Mattiuccio Salvucci (1612). To the right, in a low niche, there is a representation of the Immaculate Conception by Francesco Appiani of Perugia (18th century). The decorations in the nave, on the columns and intrados of the arches are the work of Bassotti, Amedei, Mazzi and Appiani. Originally, the lunettes above the cornice of the nave were also painted.

Beginning from the south aisle, the first altar, the Altar of the Crucifix, possesses a wealth of monumental architectural perspectives in multi-coloured marble, attributed to Vincenzo Roscino (1600). On the left-hand side, a doorway leads into the Oratory of the Brotherhood of the Crucifix. This Brotherhood built its seat between the church and the convent around the year, 1581.

The vault is decorated with false archi-

The «New» church of St. Mary: the Alessian Bell tower (17th century)

Interior (16th century)

tectural perspectives by Pietro Carattoli; in the centre, we see the Glory of the Cross by Anton Maria Garbi (1750). The altar was designed by Valentino Martelli in 1593 and was once host to the Deposition from the Cross by Felice Pellegrini (1592-93), which is now situated above the door leading into the Sacristy.

Going back into the nave, the next altar is the Altar of the Banner. It contains the processional banner by Benedetto Bonfigli (1471) which depicts the Virgin Mary and SS Benedict, Scolastic and Paolino Bigazzini imploring mercy for the people, whilst the angry figure of Jesus hurls thunderbolts onto the towered city of Perugia. The following altar is named after the Company of St. Juliana of the Lombards and originally contained an altar-piece by Andrea di Asssi which has since disappeared. The Chapel of Our Lady of Sorrows comes next. This was built in 1568 and restored in 1608. The 18th-century altar has now replaced the original one, which is thought to have the work of Martelli. In was once host to the

Deposition by Stefano Amadei which is today situated in the south transept beside the Oltramontani altar. Amadei also painted the Presentation of Mary in the Temple and the Espousal, as well as the two small canvases on the intrados of the arch — Jesus Crowned with Thorns and St. Paul the Hermit. Corresponding to the original columns of the naves, we find a pulpit dating from the mid-1500's with a canopy painted with grotesques by Mattiuccio Salvucci. Entering the transept, the first altar on the right is named after of Oltramontani Company, which moved here after leaving the Church of St. Mary of the Servants. Two niches on the side walls contain statues of St. Louis of France and St. Henry of Germany (17th century). The altar-piece depicting St. Helen worshipping the Cross is the work of Bernardino Gagliardi (18th century). There follows a door which leads into the Sacristy and Convent; above, we see the aforementioned painting by Felice Pellegrini, signed and dated by the artist (1593). The chapel at the far end contains traces of

Benedetto Bonfigli: Banner (15th century)

15th-century frescoes and of the wooden arch of Braccio I Baglioni (+ 1479). Entering the gothic apse with its ribbed vault we admire the splendid wooden choir in the international gothic style, made in 1456, by Paolino di Giovanni of Ascoli and Giovanni da Montelparo, both from the Marches region of Italy. The chapel on the left-hand side of the apse conserves fragmented frescoes depicting the Crucifixion and scenes from the life of St. Catherine by Lazzaro Vasari, great grandfather of Giorgio (15th century). Immediately next to this, there is a niche containing the figure of Christ between St. Bernardino and Stephen originating from the Umbrian school or fhe 15th century. At the head of the north transept, there is a 15th-century, carved and gold-plated altar. The altar-piece depicting the Virgin in Glory with SS. John the Baptist, Philip Neri and Philip Benizi is by Francesco Appiani (1740) and substitutes the fine Banner by Niccolò Alunno (1466), today situated in the Umbrian National Gallery. In the niche at the beginning of the aisle, there is a Virgin and Child between SS. Antony Abbot and Philip Benizi, signed by Scilla Piccinini (1585). The following altar (of the Madonna) is luxuriously carved and gold-plated (18th century) and is host to a Madonna and Child with SS. Peter and Paul, traditionally attributed to Iacopino del Conte but today thought to be the work of Girolamo Siciolante of Sermoneta (16th century). Above the side-door is an interesting painting of the Adoration of the Shepherds, probably the work of a Flemish artist (16th century). There follows the altar of the Seven Founders of the Order of Our Lady of the Servants above which a copy has been placed of the Madonna between SS. Jerome and Francis by Perugino (1507), today housed in the National Gallery in London. The copy was painted by Giuseppe Carattoli during the 19th century. The next altar is named after St. Pellegrino and contains a canvas by Francesco Appiani depicting Jesus detaching himself

Wooden Choir (15th century)

134

Cloister and bell tower

from the Cross and going to meet St. Pellegrino and St. Juliana Falconieri. The small chapel at the far end is decorated with pleasant Mannerist-style stuccowork dating from the late 16th century and contains a Madonna of Grace from the 15th-century Perugian school of painting.

Still at the end of Via del Roscetto, opposite S. Maria Nuova, we find the **Oratory of the Benedectine Brotherhood** which already existed as early as 1320. Its present form dates back to a 16th century reconstruction by Valentino Martelli (1598).

The interior still preserved the pictorial decorations of the vault (1610 circa) by Mattiuccio Salvucci (scenes from the lives of St. John the Baptist and St. Benedict) and on the lunettes (1665), by Giovan Francesco Bassotti and Giovan Battista Mazzi (scenes from the Old Testament).

From S. Maria Nuova, we may turn left into Via Pinturicchio. Inside no. 87, we find a 16th century cloister with laterite arches supported by travertine columns. This was part of the cloister of the now demolished Convent of the Servants. The bell-tower was begun in 1644 and built to a design by Galeazzo Alessi. At no. 62, we find the ancient **Monastery of St. Thomas** — first documented in 1274 — which originally belonged to the Cistercians but

135

The Oratory of St. Benedict: Matteuccio Salvucci. A detail of the Frescoes on the vault (17th century)

was passed into the hands of the Benedictine nuns from the mid-16th century on; in the period of suppression following the Unification it was converted to secular use. Of the monastery's church, there remains only the bell-tower in laterite stone.

At no. 47, we can see Pinturicchio's house and at no. 1, a lid of an Etruscan cinerary urn is visible. Via Pinturicchio leads into Piazza Fortebracci dominated by the Etruscan Arch and the Seat of the Foreign University.

Tei Arch

If we turn right at the Church of S. Maria Nuova, beyond the Tei arch and immediately on our left, we find the beginning of Corso Bersaglieri which runs alongside the mediaeval wall. After the crossroad with Via della Formica, at no.

31, we come across the former **Oratory of St. John the Baptist**, seat of this Brotherhood from 1536 onwards. The building was restored in 1705 (see inscription above the entrance). It contains a canvas by Giovanni Francesco Bassotti (17th century) depicting the bird of St. John the Baptist. A little further ahead on the left (nos. 90 and 92) there is the former Oratory of the Brotherhood of St. Antony Abbot (18th century), today used as a carpentary workshop. This brotherhood already existed in 1337.

The Church of St. Antony Abbot

Almost at the end of the street, on the right (nos. 101-102), is the **Church of St. Antony Abbot**, already a parish church in 1285. Traces of the mediaeval building are still evident in the façade and along the north flank. The church underwent its first transformation around 1450. Signs of these modificatons are visible in the fragments of Renaissance columns to be seen in the small cloister opposite the façade. A second renovation, sponsored by the Olivetans who took over the church in 1624-25, endowed the church with its present-day appearance. The loggia at the front of the building dates from the 18th century. The aisleless, barrel-vaulted interior conserves a beautiful organ in carved wood by Michele Buti of Pisa (1665); a canvas by Paolo Gismondi of Cortona (17th century) depicting St. Antony Abbot (now above the left altar, originally situated above the main altar); a 17th-century canvas by Benedetto Bandiera depicting the Child Mary and St. Anne (altar on the right); and four canvases portraying the Four Evangelists in the Presbytery area. The far wall bears frescoes by Gerardo Dottori (20th century). The Sacristy contains a rather damaged lunette painted in the 16th-century Perugian style as well as a canvas by Giovanni Andrea Carlone (1675 circa) depicting the Blessed Bernard Tolomei receiving the Habit and Rule from St. Benedict da Guido, Bishop of Arezzo. The church used to contain ten canvases by the same artist, as well as three small paintings which were incorporated into the organ display. They were, however, moved to the Church of the Olivetans od Perugia and, therefore, were finally transferred to Rome (1822).

Going back into Corso Bersaglieri, alongside the church, is a small piazza containing a drum of a Roman column upon which is placed a stone pig (15th century), the symbol of St. Antony Abbot. It is thought that it also marked the point of access to the east wing of the Monmaggiore fortress which extended almost as far as the hill of Monteluce. This was the gate through which the Piedmont army of Manfredi Fanti entered Perugia in September 1859, in oder to liberate the city of Papal domination, defeating the Papal governor Schmid, who had been responsible for the Perugia Massacre on June 20th 1859).

Beyond porta St. Antony, we can turn into Via S. Giuseppe in order to admire the final section of the mediaeval wall and the north-west slopes of the city. On the left, about 200 metres further on, we come to the little **Church of St. Joseph** (nos. 18-20), built in 1695, as is evident from the inscription above the architrave.

Continuing our tour along a lengthy avenue, we reach the present-day Convent of the **Poor Clares of Monteluce**. This was the seat of the Sylvestrine monks from 1267 onwards, after the side had been donated to St. Sylvester Guzzolini, founder of the movement. During the 17th century, after the Sylvestrine Order had left (1640-41), the area was incorporated into the property of the Oddi family and the church became a private chapel. In 1662, it adopted the name of St. Erminio, after the reliques of this saint had been transferred there. At the beginning of the 1900's, it was taken over by the Poor Clares of Monteluce.

The Church of St. Mary of Monteluce

Turning right after the porta, we find ourselves in Via Cialdini which runs alongside the laterite wall of the 16th-century reconstruction of the Rocca of Monmaggiore, attributed to Rocco di Vicenza (1519). At the end of this road, on the right, a small staircase takes us into Piazza di Monteluce where the remains are visible of three mediaeval shops in sandstone. An entire side of the Piazza is occupied by the **Church and former Convent of St. Mary of Monteluce**.

In 1281, Glotto Monaldi donated to Cardinal Ugolino, the future Gregory IX, a piece of land in the locality of Monteluce so that he could erect a church there as well as a convent and a residence for several women already living in the area. This was the official birth of the convent of St. Mary of Monteluce which was composed of a group of women following the example of St. Clare of Assisi and her companions. In the same year, Cardinal John of Perugia granted authorisation to build a church and convent. In 1219, Cardinal Ugolino ratified the convent, then in the process of being built; 1221 saw the papal confirmation of the convent by Pope Onorio III; in 1229, it was confirmed again by Gregory IX (former Cardinal Ugolino). Proof that the convent was governed by the spiritual example of the Poor Clares, is provided a *privilegian paupertatis* granted to the convent by Gregory IX, also in 1229. Notwithstan-

ding this privilege, the difficulties of monastic life made it necessary for the convent to accept the burden of property and, in 1231, Gregory IX donated some land to the nuns. From this time on, St. Mary of Monteluce acquired more and more property and possessions to the extent that, during the 15th century, the convent became the owner of an extremely large patrimony. This wealth, however, did not detract from the spiritual devotion which animated the nuns of this establishment: in 1235 and 1239, Gregory IX awarded it the Order of St. Damian which placed the convent — although the *privilegium paupertatis* of 1229 was already adequate proof of this — firmly within the framework of the Franciscan movement. The importance of the convent increased throughout the 13th century as is proved by the conspicuous number of let-

Mediaeval shops

ters and privileges issues bu Popes Inno-
cente IV, Alexander IV, Clement IV, Nicolò IV and Boniface VIII. During the
14th and 15th centuries, the convent traversed a period of moral and spiritual decadence from which it was eventually re-
deemed by drastic reforms backed by the
firm support of the city's population and
probably sponsored by St. John of Capestrano who stayed in Perugia during this
period. In 1448, a group of Poor Calres
from the already reformed convent of St.
Lucy at Foligno came to Monteluce: this
marked a new era in the convent's history
characterised by religious fervour and
also by cultural learning since it became
the seat of a *scriptorium*. During the
course of the 16th, 17th and 18th centuries, the convent of St. Mary of Monteluce was one of the richest and most prestigious religious establishments in the area
whilst maintaining a constant and high
level of moral rigour. In 1703, the spiritual
rule of the convent passed from the hands
of the Franciscan Observants into those
of the Bishop, ie. the regular clergy of the
diocese. Following the requisition of the
convent in order to convert it into a hospital
(early 20th century), the sisters moved to
the Church of St. Erminio (formerly St.
Benedict's).

The façade which almost certainly belongs to the era of its renovation (1451),
still preserves the mediaeval portal with a
rounded arch and rows of little columns
in the splays. It is covered with the chec-
kered pattern composed of different co-
loured marble which is so typical of Perugian churches. Placed in correspondence
to the bell-tower and in line with the façade wall, there is a small chapel with ancient frescoes by Anton Maria Fabrizi.
Towards the end of the 19th century, it
accomodated two canvases by Marcello
Leopardi which are now no longer trace-
able. The springers of the twin doors bear
interesting late-Mannerist carvings (late-
16th century - early-17th century) depicting Our Lady, St. CLare, St. Francis and
St. Bernardino.

The walls of the aisleless interior are entirely convered by a cycle of paintings executed probably between 1602 and 1607.

◀ **The Church of St. Mary of Monteluce**

**Anonymous artist: the Figure of an Angel
(17th century)**

They constitute an extremely interesting
iconographical ensemble of Franciscan
themes and subjects and it represents one
of the best examples of Perugian Mannerism to be seen in the city. Although local
sources tend to credit this work to Francesco Vanni and Giovanni Maria Bisconti,
the poor condition of the frescoes prevent
us from being able to advance a really
convincing hypothesis as to the actual authors; this is even more difficult, when we
bear in mind the greatly varied stylistic
methods involved.

The upper façade wall shows the Descent of the Holy Ghost, the Last supper
and the three appearances of Jesus to his
mother, the disciples and to Mary Magdalen. The lunettes of the vault are occupied
by frescoes showing episodes from the
Passion of Christ: beginning from the
right-hand wall, they are the Agony in the
Garden, the Arrest of Christ, Calvary, the
Deposition, the Resurrection and the
Ascension. In the first chapel on the right,
the intradosso of the arch is decorated
with images of the Prophets Isiah and Je-
remiah, of Louis of Toulouse and Ludovic of Angiò, St. James della Marca a St.
Pasquale Baylon. On the far wall, framed
by false architectural cornices, we find

141

paintings of St. John of Capestrano (left) and St. John of Alcantara (right); in the centre, we see a detached fresco of the Crucifixion, attributed to Fiorenzo di Lorenzo (late-15th century). Above this, a miracle of St. Antony of Padua is depicted (a horse kneeling before the Eucharist). The second chapel, with the form of a concave niche, the upper section is occupied by the symbol of the name of Jesus immediately beneath this in the centre, we see St. Francis with the Sultan with the Funeral of the Saint, on the right, and the Glory of St. Francis and St. Clare, on the left; Blessed Agidio and Blessed Antony of Stroncone are depicted within circular frames; further down again, we see SS. Cosma and Damian and the date, 1602; the central section was once host to a canvas depicting St. Francis, today preserved in the Sacristy. In the third chapel, the intrados of the arch bears the figures of St. Louis IX of France and St. Elizabeth of Hungary, on either side of the symbol of the Holy Spirit. Immediately beneath this, we see St. Louis of Toulouse (left) and St. Antony of Padua (right), St. Jerome and St. Bonaventura (left), St Augustine and St. Bernardino of Siena (right). The far wall is occupied by a Crucifixion (the Crucifix in painted wood today hangs in front the Presbytery) between Mary and St. John. Above this, is the image of the Eternal Father between Faith and Hope. St. Francis and St. Clare are framed by false architectural perspectives. All the pendetives which link the curves of the niches to the base of the lunettes are decorated with Sybils. The presbytery, occupied in the centre by the main altar with pink marble and small gothic arches (13th century), contains a prospective decoration in stucco and gold-plated wood by Valentino Carattoli (18th century). The pain-

Anonymous artist: God the Father among the Angels (17th century)

ting depicting the Coronation of the Virgin is a 19th-century copy of the original by Giulio Romano and Giovan Francesco Penni, today in the Vatican Art Gallery. It was based on a drawing by Raphael and was painted in 1524-25. The predella, attributed to Berto di Giovanni, is today in the Umbrian National Gallery. On the right towards the base, there is a fine marble tabernacle by Francesco di Simone of Fiesole depicting the Eternal Father among the angels (1487). Continuing our tour of the church, the first chapel on the right has, on the intrados, the figures of the Eternal Father, the Four Evangelists and the Four Doctors of the Church; above a niche containing a modern statue of the Madonna, we see a Nativity of the Virgin between the figures of Solomon and Isiah. On either side, there are images of the Archangel Gabriel and the Annunciation. The second chapel has the form of a concave niche. Its upper section is occupied by a fresco depicting the martyrdom of SS. Cosma and Damian. Lower down, among various figures of angels painted in chiaroscuro effects, we see the figures of St. Lucy and St. Catherine. The central section was once host to a canvas by Benedetto Cavallucci (18th century) depicting the Archangel Michael casting Satan out of Heaven, which is now situated on the inner-façade wall. The third chapel contains traces of 14th century frescoes. The intrados is decorated with angels in various attitudes. Lower down, are the images of St. Romuald and St. Antony Abbot. The altar was once host to a canvas by Benedetto Cavallucci (18th century), depicting St. Antony of Padua with Baby Jesus which has also been trasferred to the inner-façade wall. Immediately above, there is a section showing St. Bonaventura with a chorus of angels and St. John the Evangelist and Mary Magdelen. The pendetives linking the niches to the base of the lunettes are decorate by figures of the Prophets.

At the far end of the church, a small door leads into the Sacristy, a large square-shaped ambient with a ribbed cross-vault. It was once the choir of the nuns. The shorter wall towards the church is decorated with 17th-century frescoes depicting the Flagellation and the Derision of Christ. A central niche contains a small carved wooden crucifix. Beneath

Anonymous artist: St. Cosma (17th century)

this, we see images of saints and the Coronation of Our Lady (14th century). The long wall presents a series of 14th-century votive frescoes. From left to right they are: the Stigmata of St. Francis, St. Onofrio the Hermit, St. Michael the Archangel, the Baptism of Christ and four episodes from the life of St. Catherine (?) (the last two are much damaged). Traces of frescoes are also visible on the wall section immediately above this. Among the paintings hung on the walls, are the follo-

Anonymous artist: St. Francis before the Sultan (17th century)

wing: the Stigmata of St. Francis (17th century), a Glory of the Virgin and Saints (18th century) and a copy of Giulio Romano's Holy Family.

On leaving the church, we turn left into Via del Giochetto from which we can observe the side-wall of the same with its protruding buttresses, made in sandstone, in an architectural style similar to that of the Church of St. Bevignate and, outside Perugia, the Church of Montelabate. In the area opposite the church, the seasonal August Fair was held.

From Via del Giochetto we turn into Via del Favarone where, at no. 5, we find the **Convent of St. Paul of Favarone**. In 1264, this was private oratory for those who wished to pray for forgiveness. In 1317, it was presided over by a community of Sisters of Penitence which, in 1329,

embraced the rule of St. Clare, thus constituting the Convent of Poor Clares which, in 1445, merged with the convent of St. Mary of Monteluce; this merger was revoked in 1447 but confimed in 1451. The Convent then became a place of retreat for the spiritual exercises promoted by the Jesuit fathers and by the Mission; after this, it became a holiday centre for seminary students. To this end, the building was renovated in 1790, to a design by Alessio Lorenzini. At present it is a private house. A trilobal gothic doorway is all that remains of the old building.

Continuing along Via del Giochetto, we arrive in Via Enrico Del Pozzo. The area occupied by the neurological clinic was the site of a Benedictine convent named after St. Cecilia, already established in 1279. In the 1570's, the semi-derelict convent was taken over by the Capuchins who built a monastery there: hence the name «*The New Seat of the Capuchin Friars*».

Going down Via E. Dal Pozzo, at no. 101, we see the Gate of the Lion which was designed by Galeazzo Alessi as an entrance to a suburban villa belonging to him.

The Church of St. Bevignate

Further ahead, is the **Church of St. Bevignate**. Who St. Bevignate actually was is no longer historically certifiable; local tradition has it that he was a hermit; it is certain that, from 1260 to 1300, frequent requests were made by the Commune's Council for the canonisation of this saint; this local cult was not officially recognised until 1605 by the Congregation of Rites. In 1243, the site was occupied by the Templar sect; work was begun on the building (at least as regards planning and design) in 1256; in 1283, the church was consacrated. It was built on or beside the site of a previous chapel named after St. Jerome. In 1312, following the suppression of the Templars, the church was taken over by the Knights of St. John of Jerusalem. Between 1324 and 1327, a female community adherring to the Order of St. John moved there; in 1517, the sisters left and the church returned into the hands of the Knights of St. John of Jerusalem, who let it 'in commenda'. It gradually became a simple Abbey dependency of the Holy See. In 1860, it was secularised.

The double-skewed façade, bound by two robust buttresses, has a travertine round-archade doorway and a moulded rose-window. The north flank is similar in style to the architecture of St. Mary of Monteluce and St. Mary of Valdiponte or Montelabate (near Perugia) and has a side door terminating in an ogival arch.

The aisleless interior is divided into two areas by ogival cross-vaults. It may originally have had a tie-beamed ceiling similar to the one above the vault of St. Mary of Monteluce. The square-shaped apse also has a ribbed cross-vault and is illuminated by a large ogival mullioned window in travertine. Here, we find the oldest painting of the church, executed by local artists during the 1760's. The upper left section of the far wall shows a Madonna and child with thurifer angels; on the right, the apostles Philip, James and Tho-

The Church of St. Bevignate

mas are depicted. The central area, on the sides of the mullioned window, is occupied by the symbol of the Four Evangelists. The symbol of Luke is partially superimposed by the figure of St. Paul which belongs to the pictorial series reprsenting the Apostles which runs along the main wall. At the centre of the lower fascia, the Crucifix between the Virgin Mary and St. John is depicted; left and right of this, two scenes from the life of St. Bevignate are depicted (in the much-damaged first one, we see the Saint obtaining the permission of the Bishop of Perugia to live in the forest; in the second, the Bishop authorises the saint to take the Hermit's cowl). The right-hand wall of the apse is occupied by the scene of the Day of Judgement. Christ the Judge, surrounded by nine Apostles (seven in the upper section and two in the lower) is represented seated on a throne between the symbols of his Passion. On either side, an angel blows the trumpet of justice. Beneath this, is depicted a rare and interesting representation of the Blest and the Damned; the former look towards Christ in supplication; the latter look out of stone tombs. Lower down again, we see an interesting pictorial representation of the Flagellants chasing eachother with whips. A votive fresco originating from a later epoch (14th century) depicting St. Bevignate in the act of blessing, interrupts this series of figures. The left-hand wall, with a single-lighted window, bears only poor traces of painting. To the right of the large window, there is a vulgar rendering of the Madonna; above this, large fragments of a Last Supper can be seen (Christ in the act of blessing, six Apostles and a man kneeling in front of the table). The lower fascia once depicted an episode from the life of St. Bevignate, today almost invisible. Left and right of this, we can still see the images of St. Lawrence in a red tunic and St. Stephen in a white tunic. Along the wall of the nave, the figures of the Apostles are arranged with large spaces between each. They are the work of a refined Byzantine-style painter (late 13th century), thought by some to appertain to the Roman school though others believe he may have originated from Lombardy. The left-hand pier of the triumphal arch bears a fragmented Crucifix dating back to the 14th century. The left-hand wall of

the first section shows images of St. Clare of Montefalco and St. Francis (early-15th century) next to a St. Mary Magdalen dating back to the 14th century. Above this, a rich decorative frieze runs the course of the entire wall of the church. It incorporates geometrical motifs, symbols and heraldic emblems and is thought to be the work of a local artist living during the late-13th century. The same artist was also author of the paintings in the two large lunettes located, one above the other, on the inner-façade wall. The first one, depicting scenes of battles between the Templars and Saracens, are of particular historical and religious interest.

Next door to the Church of St. Bevignate is a house with architectural forms similar to those of the Library of Monteripido.

The monumental **Cemetery of Perugia** is a short way ahead on the right. It was Gioacchino Pecci (the future Pope Leone XIII) who strongly promoted — after the governement decree of 1836 — the construction of the cemetery, notwithstanding the strong opposition of the nobility and most of the town's bourgeoisie. The Innauguartion took place on November 23rd 1849. The first project was designed by the communal engineer, Filippo Lardoni (1849), a second project for its extension was the work of Alessandro Arienti from Milan. The original cemetery already contained several monumental works of considerable architectural complexity, among which the following are of particular note: the sepulchral monuments of Prof. Lorenzo Massini by Raffaele Carattoli, son of Luigi; the tomb of the little Buattini child by Raffaele Carattoli and Raffaele Omicini; the tomb of the noblewoman, Francesca Perucchini by Giuseppe Luchetti; and of the Marquis Glotto Monaldi by Guglielmo Ciani, a pupil of Bartolini in Florence. After the enlargement of the cemetery, other impressive monuments were built, mainly by Francesco Biscarini and Raffaele Angeletti who, at the end of the century, opened a terracotta factory. Among the other numerous sculptors involved, are the following: Giuseppe Frenguelli, Romano Mignini, Enrico Quattrini, Giuseppe Scardovi and Angelo Biscarini. Among the architects, the following are of particular importance: Nazzareno Biscarini, Guglielmo Calderini, Edoardo Vignaroli and Ulpiano Bucci, designer of the Majestic mausoleum of the Cesaroni family.

Further on, near the entrance of the new cemetery, is the **Church of St. Mary of Grace of Monterone**, designed in 1534 by Brother Giordano Tassi, in a sober and elegant style similar to that of the church of St. Mary of Light near porta St. Susanna. The façade, with travertine ashlarwork, is bordered on the sides by two pillars upon which rests a tympanum. There is a rose-window with elegant decorative motifs above the door.

On the return journey, we continue along Via Enrico Dal Pozzo which leads us through a zone knows as Fontenuova as early as the 13th century; event today, a fountain, clearly incorporating mediaeval fragments, is still visible. It was in the locality of Fontenuovo that Raniero Fasani, father of the Discipline Movement attempted to establish his oratory. Further ahead, where there now exists a marble workshop, was the site of the hospital church of the Shoemakers Guild, named after St. Crispino. It is possible that the hospital existed as early as the 15th century; in 1737, it was combined with the large hospital of St. Mary of Mercy and, on this occasion the building was restored and enlarged. Today, we can admire its well-composed façade in white and red stone with a slender cornice composed of small medallions.

The Church of St. Simon of Carmine

At the end of Via Enrico Del Pozzo, we pass under an archway and enter Via dell'Asilo, once again among the tangle of narrow and characteristic city streets. After a brief stretch, we find the **Church of St. Simon of Carmine**, a parish church as early as 1285 and, without doubt, existing as early as 1233. According to Siepi, in 1296, it was donated to the Carmelites by the Bishop of Perugia.

The church's exterior bears numerous signs of the renovation works carried out at a various stages in its history: 1571, 1636, 1746 and 1852. Interesting traces of the mediaeval building are visible on the flank of the church (in Via Abruzzo) where we can see the exterior wall of a

gothic chapel with a single-lighted travertine window. The aisleless barrel vaulted interior — in its present form — belongs to the 19th-century renovation which completely transformed the decoration of the chapel and vaults, painted during the 16th and early-17th centuries by Simeone Ciburri, Cesare Sermei and Anton Maria Fabrizi. Backing onto the innerfaçade wall is an organ dated 1602 with carved figures in the late-Mannerist style depicting Saints of the Carmelite Order. The first altar on the right has a canvas depicting St. Andrew Corsini by Anton Maria Fabrizi (17th century). The second is host to a painting of St. Albert by Avanzino Nucci (1607). The following altar, dedicated to the Della Corgna family, is host to a Crucifix in carved multicoloured wood by Leonard Scaglia (17th century). A niche in the centre contains a small processional banner of the Bonfigli school (15th century). Going back into the nave, the second altar on the right has

The Church of Carmine: a view of the left flank as seen from Via Abruzzo

a canvas by Anton Maria Fabrizi depicting the Madonna and Child with St. Mary Magdalen of the Mad and the titular saints Simon and Jude. The first altar has a canvas showing St. Elijah by a 17th century local artist. Finally, the four confessionals made of carved walnut are of considerable quality. The sacristy contains several canvases including a St. Jerome of the Ribera school (17th century) and a Mystic Espousal of St. Catherine, in the style of Avanzino Nucci (17th century). Also of interest in a series of lunettes depicting the history of the Carmelite Order and its personages, by a local artist working around the middle 17th century in a style very similar to that of Anton Maria Fabrizi. The same artist was also author of the paintings at the centre of the vault depicting the Madonna and Child and St. Michael the Archangel. The ancient refectory (now part of the 'Santa Croce' nursery school in Via dell'Asilo no. 1) contains five lunettes depicting episodes from the story of the Prophet Elias by Anton Maria Fabrizi (17th century).

A short way beyond, we come to the **Oratory of the Brotherhood of SS. Simon and Fiorenzo** (Via Imbriani no. 41/b). The Brotherhood of St. Fiorenzo — near to the church and monastery of the name — already existed in 1337; that of St. Simon was officially established in 1371, although there is evidence of it having already existed in the 1340's. These two brotherhoods merged sometime before 1571. The interior, the vault of which was originally decorated with frescoes by Pietro Carattoli (1724), has, above the altar, an interesting painting by Pietro Montanini (1674), depicting the Madonna and Child with SS. Simon, Fiorenzo, Francis and Antony.

Opposite the Church of St. Simon del Carmine, a flight of stairs takes us into the small piazza del Duca, which takes its name from the presence of an impressive palazzo belonging to the Dukes of Corgna (late-16th century).

Taking Via Imbriani, we can stop off in Via S. Giovanni del Fosso where, at no. 13, we see the former parish church of the same name, which was established in 1233. Over the centuries, the church was renovated several times. From Via S. Giovanni del Fosso, we enter into Via della Viola and, a short distance ahead, we find the begining of Via della Pazienza, where we can see the ancient Etruscan/Roman city wall in hewn travertine with evidence of a mediaeval restoration (1308) employing diverse materials (travertine, calcareous rock, sandstone and laterite).

If we walk to the end of Via Imbriani, before going up Via Alessi, we can turn into Via Bonaccia which leads us under the mediaeval Gate of St. Margaret; nearby, we can see traces of the mediaeval wall, even if this particular stretch has undergone drastic transformation. This was one of the steepest slopes of Perugia and, therefore, had need of frequent repair. The area opposite the gate — now occupied by the Psychiatric Hospital — was once the site of the Benedictine Convent of St. Margaret. The «domine ecclesie Sancte Margerite» was first metioned in a document of 1248; the convent was among those protected by the communal authorities, as stated in the statue of 1279. It was suppressed in 1810.

The Church of St. Fiorenzo

At the cross-road of Via Imbriani, Via Alessi and Via della Viola, we find the **Church and Former Monastery of St. Fiorenzo**.

This building, named after St. Fiorenzo the martyr, has very remote origins (8th century?). From the 11th century on, it belonged to the Abbey of St. Salvatore of Monte Acuto. When the abbey near Perugia was reformed, passing into the hands of the Cistercians, the monastery of St. Fiorenzo followed suit. During the 1440's, Eugene IV introduced there the Servants of Mary, thus eliminating all Cistercian influence and all forms of dependence on St. Salvatore of Monte Acuto.

The church was originally built in the gothic style; a few traces of this remain on the exterior: the foundations of the belltower, a small chapel with a single-arched window and several adjacent rooms. It was completely renovated during the second half of the 18th century to a design by Pietro Carattoli (1768-70). the aisleless interior has — on the inner-façade wall — detached frescoes taken from the room next to the 16th-century cloister (others are preserved in a gothic hall parallel to the side wall of the church and in the parish office). Above the side-door, there is

Cloister of the former Monastery of St. Fiorenzo

a 15th-century style painting by Giustino Cristofani (early-20th century). The first altar on the right by Francesco Appiani (18th century) depicts St. Pellegrino supported by an angel and Blessed John Porro. Backing onto the canvas, is a carved wooden Crucifix. The second altar which once belonged to the Ansidei family is host to a copy by Nicola Monti (18th century) of the famous altar-piece by Raphael (today in the National Gallery in London), which was located in the church up to 1764. Above the first altar on the left, we find a canvas by Francesco Appiani (18th century), depicting the Miracle of the Host of St. Juliana Falconieri. Opposite the second chapel, a fragment of a 15th-century fresco, part of the former decoration of the church, is still visible (15th century). The altar in the south arm of the transept has an interesting banner dated 1476, attributed to Benedetto Bonfigli, depicting an enraged Jesus with the beseeching figures of the Virgin and SS.

Benedetto Bonfigli: Banner (15th century) ▶

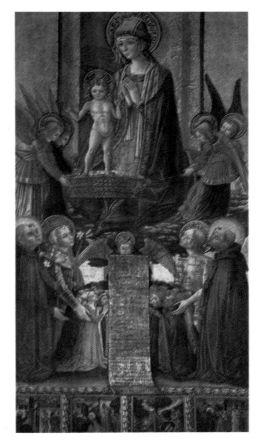

Anton Maria Fabrizi: Frescoes in the Sacristy (17th century)

Matteuccio Salvucci: Frescoes in the Sacristy (17th century)

Philip Benizi, Fiorenzo and Pellegrino Leziosi whilst an angel shows the penitent people a scroll on which is written a long reproof, the text of which is attributed to Spirito Gualtieri or Coppetta, both poets from Perugia. Below this, four episodes from the life of St. Philip Benizi are depicted. A niche in the centre of the presbytery contains a 14th-century fresco taken from the nearby Vicolo della Madonna in 1770 and restored in 1815 by Carlo Labrussi. The altar of the north transept, in stucco work by Benetto Silva (18th century), who also made the Banner altar, is host to a canvas by Francesco Silva (18th century) depicting the Virgin among the clouds and the seven Blessed Founders. The Sacristy contains interesting wardrobes dating back to the 17th century; it also has paintings on the lunettes depicting episodes from the life of St. Lawrence which are partly the work of Matteuccio Salvucci (1612) and partly (the right-hand wall) by Anton Maria Fabrizi (1630).

Returning along Via Alessi, we find ourselves back in Piazza Matteotti.

The Etruscan Hypogeums

The Hypogeums of San Manno

The Etruscan hypogeum of San Manno is situated at about two kilometres from the station of Perugia on the road leading to Florence (Via Cortonese - Ferro di Cavallo). Since mediaeval times, this hypo-geum has been incorporated in the surrounding area of the tower/house and a small chapel dedicated to St. Manno. This chapel still contains traces of the pictorial decoration of the apse (14th century) and a fresco (Madonna and Child between St. John the Baptist and St. Manno), dated and signed by Silla Piccinini (1585).

The hypogeum which dates back to the second century B.C. is part of the necropolis which developed in the general area of Porta Eburnea — San Manno — Cortona. A subject of profound research since the end of the last century, it presents a characteristic Greek Cross plan with a barrel vault and is built out of slabs of travertine rock with visible armillas. The Tombs of Sagraia and that of Bettona are two other sepulchral buildings of a similar structure, both situated in the Perugian area. The occupied space follows an east-west axis; half-way along each wall, there is a burial niche, also with travertine vaults. Above the northern niche, we find an inscription lasting three lines, defined by Maffei as «the queen of Etruscan inscriptions». According to seversal scholars, it is a commemorative inscription of the brothers, Lartre and Aule Preca whose family had built the hypogeum for them. Recent studies on the monument have established that the original entrance to the tomb and *dromos* were probably located in the west wall, opposite, that is, to the present entrance.

The Volumnian Hypogeum

The Volumnian Hypogeum is situated at about seven kilometres from the town centre in the direction of Assisi along the State Road 75 bis, near the locality of Ponte San Giovanni. It represents part of the Palazzone necropolis which occupies hill lying behind. The numerous tombs of this necropolis have the form of chambers dug directly into the volcanic rock. Most of the materials of the corredos belong to the Hellenistic era although some objects date from the fourth century B.C.

The 19th-century vestibule of the hypogeum contains numerous cinerary urns, mostly in travertine, but also in terracotta, marble and sandstone. The travertine urns are of the architectural type with double-skewed lids, inscriptions of the tympanum, and relief work with traces of colour on the front. The subjects of the decorations are mainly mythological in type. Several of the lids have the reclining figure of the deceased on them. A room to the right of the entrance displays various pieces of ceramic work (mainly in terracotta) taken from the necropolis during excavations carried out during the 19th century.

A steep staircase, dug into the sandy conglomerate rock, leads down to the sepulchral chamber. The doorway is made of robust travertine jambs, an architrave with a rock slab to close the entrance, and bears a vertical inscription on the right commemorating the date of the hypohypogeum, built by Arunte and Lars Volimnio. The interior is subdivided into different spaces, according to a scheme similar to that used in the Roman/Italic house (atrium, tablinum and cubicola).

The atrium has a double-skewed ceiling imitating the beams of a wooden covering. The central beam has the figure of a genie which functions as a lamp-holder. The two pediments are decorated with the Medusa's head between two dolphins and the Medusa's head between two swords and two male busts. The tablinum has a

Volumnian Hypogeum: the Urn of Arunte Volumnio

Volumnian Hypogeum: Cinerary Urn

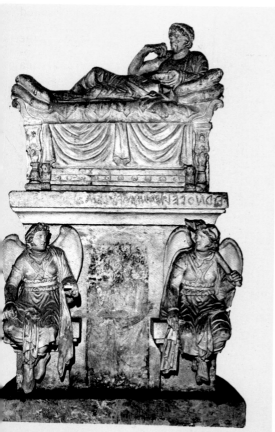

Volumnian Hypogeum: Cinerary Urn

box-ceiling (identical to the one to be found in the lateral cells), with a Medusa's head in the centre. Above the piers are seven cinerary urns: one in marble, and six in stucco-covered travertine. At the centre of the far wall, there is the important and interesting urn of Arunte Volumnio, son of Aulo; the deceased is represented in a reclining position above a *Kline* on which the Gate of Hades is depicted. Also of great artistic interest, is

the urn of Velia Volumnia, daughter of Arunte, represented in a reclining position on the urn lid. The marble urn in the form of a Roman house is, without doubt, of a later period (perhaps the Augustan era); it is the urn of Publio Volumnio, son of Aulo; the urn also bears a bi-lingual epigraph.

The exact date of the hypogeum is still uncertain. However, scholars tend to think it originates from the second century B.C.

The Villa dello Sperandio Hypogeum

Leaving Perugia from Porta S. Angelo and following, on the right, the mediaeval town wall, we take a road on the left and arrive at the Villa of the Sperandio family. In 1900, a tomb was discovered nearby, dug into the rock face at a depth of about five meters. It preserves a door with an architrave and two bronze studs. The interior once contained a travertine sarcophagus containing the remains of a woman who may have been a priestess. The precious funeral corredo was found spread all over the floor. Today these objects can be seen in the Florence Archaeological musem. Among the most interesting articles found there was a bronze mirror decorated with a winged-genie together with an Adonis. There were also two gold ear-rings, and a gold lamina tiara in the form of lanceolate leaves. In the area surrounding this hypogeum, numerous other tombs have been found, together with cinerary urns, a cremation platform and several ruins, clear proof of the existence of a necropolis.

BIBLIOGRAPHY

This bibliography does not claim to be complete. It is simply a list of the books consulted during the writing of this guide. The material has been put into categories according to them and is then listed in chronological order.

GUIDES

MORELLI G.F., *Brevi notizie delle pitture e sculture che adornano l'augusta città di Perugia*, Perugia 1683.

ORSINI B., *Guida al forestiere per l'augusta città di Perugia*, Perugia 1784.

SIEPI S., *Descrizione topologico-istorica della città di Perugia*, Perugia 1822.

GAMBINI R., *Guida di Perugia*, Perugia 1826.

MARCHESI R., *Principali monumenti d'arte in Perugia*, Perugia 1857.

ROSSI SCOTTI G.B., *Breve guida di Perugia*, Perugia 1861.

GUARDABASSI M., *Indice-guida dei monumenti pagani e cristiani... esistenti nelle provincie dell'Umbria*, Perugia 1872.

ROSSI SCOTTI G.B., *Guida illustrata di Perugia*, Perugia 1878.

LUPATELLI A., *Una settimana a Perugia. Breve guida*, Foligno 1885.

LUPATELLI A., *Petit guide de Pérouse*, Paris 1895.

GALLENGA STUART R.A., *Perugia*, Bergamo 1907.

BRIGANTI A. - MAGNINI M. - LOCATELLI G., *Guida di Perugia*, Perugia 1907.

LUPATELLI A., *Guida illustrata di Perugia*, Perugia 1909.

RIZZATTI F., *Perugia*, Bologna 1911.

RIZZATTI F., *Tre giorni a Perugia*, Perugia 1913.

BOMBE W., *Perugia*, Leipsig 1914.

SCHNEIDER R., *Pérouse*, Paris 1914.

MAGNINI M. - BRIGANTI A., *Guida di Perugia*, Perugia 1923.

NAZZARI G.U., *La più bella tra le città minori: Perugia*, Città di Castello 1933.

CAPITINI A., *Perugia*, Firenze 1947.

SANTI F., *Perugia. Guida storico-artistica*, Perugia 1950.

BRIGANTI F., *Perugia. Guida toponomastica*, Perugia 1954.

GURRIERI O., *Perugia. Guida artistica illustrata*, Milano 1958.

BALLO A. - GURRIERI O., *Perugia*, Roma 1962.

Umbria, a cura del T.C.I., Milano 1978.

SCARPELLINI P., *Guida breve di Perugia*, Perugia 1980.

GENERAL HISTORY

CIATTI F., *Delle memorie annali et istoriche delle cose di Perugia*, Perugia 1638.

CRISPOLTI C., *Perugia Augusta*, Perugia 1648.

PELLINI P., *Dell'historia di Perugia*, 1 e 2 Venezia 1664, rist. Bologna 1968, 3, Perugia 1970.

MARIOTTI A., *Saggio di memorie istoriche, civili ed ecclesiastiche della città di Perugia e suo contado*, Perugia 1806.

VERMIGLIOLI G.B., *La vita e le imprese di Malatesta IV Baglioni*, Perugia 1839.

BARTOLI A., *Storia della città di Perugia*, Perugia 1843.

FABRETTI A., *Vita e fatti di Malatesta Baglioni*, Montepulciano 1846.

Cronache e storie inedite della città di Perugia dal MCL al MDLXIII, a cura di F. Bonaini, A. Fabretti, F.L. Polidori, in *Archivio Storico Italiano*, 1, 16 (1850); 2, 16 (1851).

BONAZZI L., *Storia di Perugia*, Perugia 1875, rist. Città di Castello 1960.

Cronache della città di Perugia, a cura di A. Fabretti, Torino 1887-92.

Documenti di storia perugina, a cura di A. Fabretti, I, Torino 1887, II, ivi 1892.

FUMI L., *Inventario e spoglio dei registri della Tesoreria Apostolica di Perugia e Umbria dal R. Archivio di Stato di Roma*, Roma 1901.

DE BAGLION DE LA DUFFERIE L., *Les Baglioni de Pérouse*, Poitiers 1907.

GIGLIARELLI R., *Perugia antica e Perugia moderna*, Perugia 1907.

HEYWOOD W., *A history of Perugia*, London 1910.

SYMONDS M. - DUFF GORDON L., *The story of Perugia*, London 1927.

CAMPANO G.A., *De vita et gestis Braccii*, a cura di R. Valentini, in RIS 19/4, 1929.

GUARDABASSI F., *Storia di Perugia*, Perugia 1933-35.

ERMINI G., *Storia dell'Università di Perugia*, Bologna 1947, 2ª ed., Firenze 1971.

BEVILACQUA E., *Perugia. Ricerche di geografia urbana*, Roma 1950.

BALEONUS ASTUR, *I Baglioni*, Firenze 1964.

ABBONDANZA R. - BELLINI L. - CAIZZI A. - CIOTTI V. - SANTI F., *Umbria*, Venezia 1970.

GURRIERI O., *Storia di Perugia*, Perugia 1979.

GROHMANN A., *Perugia*, Bari 1981.

SPECIFIC HISTORICAL SUBJECTS

MASSARI C., *Saggio storico-medico sulle pestilenze di Perugia e sul governo sanitario di esse dal sec. XIV*, Perugia 1838.

MARCHESI R., *Il cambio di Perugia*, Prato 1853.

ANSIDEI V. - GIANNANTONI L., *I codici delle sommissioni al comune di Perugia*, in *Bollettino della Deputazione di Storia Patria per l'Umbria = BDSPU*, 1 (1895), 2 (1896), 3 (1897), 4 (1898), 5 (1899), 6 (1900), 8 (1902), 9 (1903), 10 (1904), 12 (1906).

DEGLI AZZI G., *Il tumulto del 1488 in Perugia e la politica di Lorenzo il Magnifico*, in BDSPU, 11 (1905).

BRIGANTI F., *Città dominanti e comuni minori nel Medio Evo con speciale riguardo alla repubblica perugina*, Perugia 1906.

FUMI L., *L'« Iter Urbevetanum et Perusinum» del Garampi*, in BDSPU, 14 (1909).

BRIGANTI A., *Le corporazioni delle arti nel comune di Perugia (sec. XIII-XIV)*, Perugia 1910.

Statuti di Perugia dell'anno MCCCXLII, a cura di G. Degli Azzi, Milano 1913-16, libri 4.

BACILE DI CASTIGLIONE G., *La rocca Paolina di Perugia*, Perugia 1914.

LUPATTELLI A., *Il civico cimitero di Perugia nel 70° anniversario della sua costruzione e inaugurazione (1849-1919)*, Perugia 1920.

LUPATTELLI A., *I salotti perugini del secolo XIX e l'Accademia dei Filedoni*, Empoli 1921; ed. a cura di R. Trabalza, Foligno 1976.

MARINI G.B., *Cronaca 1794-1833*, in BDSPU, 31 (1933), 33 (1935), 34 (1937), 39 (1942), 51 (1954), 54 (1957), 56 (1959), 57 (1960), 58 (1961), 59 (1962), 61 (1964), 62 (1965).

ANSIDEI V., *Regestum reformationum comunis Perusii ab anno MCCLVI ad annum MCCC*, 1, Perugia 1935.

BELELLI G., *L'istituto del podestà in Perugia nel secolo XIII*, Bologna 1936.

DUPRÉ THESEIDER E., *La rivolta di Perugia nel 1375 contro l'abate di Monmaggiore ed i suoi precedenti politici*, in BDSPU, 25 (1938).

BELFORTI R., *Il Collegio della Mercanzia in Perugia e il suo Archivio*, in BDSPU, 36 (1939).

LUPATTELLI A., *L'Università per Stranieri di Perugia. 1925-1943*, Perugia 1947.

FRANCESCHINI G., *Biordo Michelotti e la dedizione di Perugia al duca di Milano*, in BDSPU, 45 (1948).

SALVATORELLI L., *La politica interna di Perugia in un poemetto volgare della metà del Trecento*, in BDSPU, 50 (1953).

MIRA G., *Aspetti dell'organizzazione corporativa in Perugia nel XIV secolo*, in *Economia e storia*, 6 (1959).

PARATORE E., *Il bimillenario della guerra di Perugia e della pace di Brindisi*, in *Studi Romani*, 8 (1960).

VITUCCI G., *Il «Bellum Perusinum» (nel bimillenario)*, in BDSPU, 57 (1960).

ABBONDANZA R., *Primi appunti sulla legislazione statutaria di Perugia dei secoli XIII e XIV*, in BDSPU, 59 (1962).

SEGOLONI D., *Bartolo da Sassoferrato e la civitas perusina*, in *Bartolo da Sassoferrato. Studi e documenti per il VI Centenario*, 2, Milano 1962.

ABBONDANZA R., voce *Braccio Baglioni*, in *Dizionario Biografico degli Italiani*, 5, Roma 1963.

FRANCESCHINI G., *La dedizione di Perugia a Gian Galeazzo Visconti Duca di Milano*, in *Archivio Storico Lombardo*, 90 (1963).

MELONI P.L., *I cattolici e la grande guerra nella pubblicistica perugina*, in *Benedetto XV, i cattolici e la prima guerra mondiale*, Roma 1963.

Annali e cronaca di Perugia in volgare dal 1191 al 1336, a cura di F.A. Ugolini, in *Annali della Facoltà di Lettere e Filosofia dell'Università di Perugia*, 1, Perugia 1964.

NICOLINI U., *Un «consilium» inedito di Guido da Suzzara e la lotta politica a Perugia al tempo di Corradino*, in *Annali di Storia del Diritto*, 8 (1964).

CALASSO F., *Bartolo da Sassoferrato*, in *Dizionario Biografico degli Italiani*, 6, Roma 1965.

CAMPANA A., *I possessi della Chiesa di Ravenna nei territori di Perugia e Gubbio*, in *Atti del II Convegno di Studi Umbri*, Perugia 1965.

PETROCCHI M., *L'ultimo destino perugino di Innocenzo III*. in BDSPU, 64 (1967).

GROHMANN A., *La Società di mutuo soccorso fra gli artisti ed operai di Perugia (1861-1900)*, in BDSPU, 65 (1968).

PECUGI FOP M., *Il comune di Perugia e la Chiesa durante il periodo avignonese con particolare riferimento all'Albornoz*, in BDSPU, 65 (1968), 66 (1969).

NICOLINI U., *Reformationes comunis Perusii quae extant anni MCCLXII*, Perugia 1969.

RANIERI DI SORBELLO U., *Perugia della Bell'Epoca*, Perugia 1969.

GALLETTI A.I., *Considerazioni per una interpretazione dell'Eulista*, in *Archivio Storico Italiano*, 128 (1970).

PAGLIACCI G., *Le matricole dell'arte della Mercanzia in Perugia*, Perugia 1970.

RICCIARELLI G., *I prototipografi in Perugia. Fonti documentarie*, in BDSPU, 67 (1970).

RONCETTI M., *Un inventario dell'archivio privato della famiglia Michelotti. Considerazioni su Biordo e i suoi fratelli*, in BDSPU, 67 (1970).

ABBONDANZA R., *Gli statuti perugini dal 1279 al 1342 e il ritrovamento del primo rilevante frammento della redazione statutaria del 1342*, in *Atti del VI Convegno di Studi Umbri*, Perugia 1971.

CECCHINI G., *Fra Bevignate e la guerra perugina contro Foligno*, Ibid.

GOLDBRUNNER H., *I rapporti tra Perugia e Milano alla fine del Trecento*, Ibid.

GRUNDMAN A., *La posizione economica della nobiltà perugina del Trecento*, Ibid.

NICOLINI U., *Le mura medievali di Perugia*, Ibid.

PETROCCHI M., *Le «sommissioni» alla città di Perugia nell'età di Federico Barbarossa*, Ibid.

ROMIZI-RICCI P., *Il notaio perugino Pietro di Lippolo e le sue «imbreviaturae» del 1348*, in *Annali della Facoltà di Lettere e Filosofia dell'Università di Perugia*, Perugia 1971.

RUTEMBURG V., *Popolo e movimenti popolari nell'Italia del '300 e '400*, trad. it., Bologna 1971.

TOSI L., *Romeo A. Gallenga Stuart e la propaganda di guerra all'estero (1917-1919)*, in *Storia Contemporanea*, 2 (1971), n. 3.

BARTOLI LANGELI A., *I documenti sulla guerra tra Perugia e Foligno del 1253-54*, in BDSPU, 69 (1972).

BLACK C., *Politica e amministrazione a Perugia tra Quattrocento e Cinquecento*, in *Atti del VII Convegno di Studi Umbri*, Perugia 1972.

GOLDBRUNNER H., *Il dominio visconteo a Perugia*, Ibid.

L'Umbria nella Resistenza, a cura di S. Bovini, Roma 1972.

BARTOCCINI F., *La lotta politica in Umbria dopo l'Unità*, in *Atti dell'VIII Convegno di Studi Umbri*, Perugia 1973.

GROHMANN A., *Primi momenti dell'Associazionismo operaio in Umbria: le società di Mutuo Soccorso*, Ibid.

Il Notariato a Perugia, a cura di R. Abbondanza, Roma 1973.

MAZZONIS F., *Correnti politiche in Umbria prima dell'Unità (1849-1860)*, in *Atti dell'VIII Convegno di Studi Umbri*, Perugia 1973.

MINCIOTTI M., *Un perugino tra due rivoluzioni: Fabio Danzetta (1769-1837)*, in BDSPU, 70 (1973).

UGOLINI R., *Cavour e Napoleone III nell'Italia centrale. Il sacrificio di Perugia*, Roma 1973.

CHIACCHELLA R., *Economia e amministazione a Perugia nel Seicento*, Reggio Calabria 1974.

FRASCARELLI F., *Nobiltà minore e borghesia a Perugia nel sec. XV*, Perugia 1974.

GALLETTI A.I., *La società comunale di fronte alla guerra nelle fonti perugine del 1282*, in BDSPU, 71 (1974).

GRUNDMAN J.P., *The popolo at Perugia (1139-1309)*, Saint-Louis, Missouri, 1974.

SALVATORELLI L., *L'insurrezione di Perugia e la politica di Cavour nell'Italia centrale*, in BDSPU, 71 (1974).

Antifascismo e Resistenza nella Provincia di Perugia, a cura di L. Cappuccelli, Roma 1975.

BISTONI U. - MONACCHIA P., *Due secoli di Massoneria a Perugia e in Umbria*, Perugia 1975.

MAGNINI D., *Questa nostra storia*, Perugia 1975.

PIEROTTI R., *Aspetti del mercato e della produzione a Perugia fra la fine del secolo XIV e la prima metà del XV*, in

BDSPU, 72 (1975), 73 (1976).

RUBIN BLANSHEI S., *Perugia, 1260-1340: Conflict and Change in a Medieval Italian Urban Society*, Philadelphia 1976.

MEZZANOTTE F., *La pace di Bologna tra Perugia e Urbano V (23 novembre 1370)*, in BDSPU, 74 (1977).

TOSI N., *Reazione agraria e origini del nazionalismo a Perugia*, in BDSPU, 74 (1977).

BRACCO F., *Note sull'opposizione al fascismo e la stampa clandestina a Perugia*, in *Politica e società in Italia dal fascismo alla Resistenza*, a cura di G. Nenci, Bologna 1978.

Cattolici e fascisti in Umbria 1922-1945, a cura di A. Monticone, Bologna 1978.

CECCHINI G., *La Biblioteca Augusta del comune di Perugia*, Roma 1978.

NERI M., *Perugia e il suo contado nei secoli XIII e XIV. Interventi urbanistici e legislazione statutaria*, in *Atti del X Convegno di Studi Umbri*, Perugia 1978.

GIUNTELLA M,C., *Il circolo universitario cattolico e l'ambiente dell'Ateneo Perugino tra le due guerre mondiali*, in *Chiesa e società dal secolo IV ai nostri giorni*, 2, Roma 1979.

TOSTI M., *La Chiesa a Perugia tra conservazione e democrazia (1798-1799)*, Ibid.

AA.VV., *La fiera dei morti di Perugia*, Perugia 1980.

AA.VV., *Per un nuovo modello di città. Progetto Perugia*, Perugia 1980.

MINCIOTTI TSOUKAS C., *La restaurazione a Perugia*, in *Atti del Convegno interregionale di Storia del Risorgimento. «Pio VII e il card. Consalvi: un tentativo di riforma nello Stato Pontificio»*, Viterbo 1980.

MINCIOTTI TSOUKAS C., *Spontaneità e brigantaggio: l'insorgenza contadina in Umbria*, Annali Cervi 2, Bologna 1980.

PORCARO M.R., *La ristrutturazione di un centro cittadino: Perugia e la demolizione della rocca Paolina*, in *Storia urbana*, 4 (1980).

AA.VV., *Ricerche su Perugia tra Due e Quattrocento*, Perugia 1981.

PIEROTTI R., *La circolazione monetaria nel territorio perugino nei secoli XII-XIV*, in BDSPU, 78 (1981).

Pozzi e cisterne medievali della città di Perugia, a cura dell'Associazione subacquea «Orsa minore», Perugia 1981.

AA.VV., *Un quartiere e la sua storia. La Conca di Perugia*, Perugia 1982.

FRASCARELLI F., *Note sulla curia papale a Perugia nel sec. XIII*, in *Annali della Facoltà di Lettere e Filosofia dell'Università di Perugia*, in corso di stampa.

GROHMANN A., *Città e territorio tra Medioevo ed Età Moderna: Perugia secc. XIII-XVI*, Perugia 1981.

GROHMANN A., *Ricchezza e potere a Perugia dall'avvento di Braccio alla guerra del sale (1416-1540)*, in *Materiali di Storia*, 4, in corso di stampa.

RELIGIOUS HYSTORY

RICCI E., *Storia della Beata Colomba da Rieti*, Perugia 1901.

CERNICCHI A., *L'acropoli sacra di Perugia e suoi archivi*, Perugia 1911.

RICCI E., *Un diploma di Federico I per il Duomo di Perugia*, in *Archivio per la Storia Ecclesiastica dell'Umbria*, 1 (1913).

LUPATTELLI A., *I primi Servi di Maria in Perugia*, Empoli 1919.

RICCIERI A., *Indice degli Annali Ecclesiastici Perugini tratto dalla Cancelleria Decemvirale*, in *Archivio per la Storia Ecclesiastica dell'Umbria*, 5 (1921).

FANTOZZI A., *Documenta Perusina de S. Bernardino Senensi*, in *Archivum Franciscanum Historicum*, 15 (1922).

AA.VV., *Il Tempio di S. Francesco al Prato in Perugia*, Perugia 1927.

LANZONI F., *Le diocesi d'Italia*, 1, Faenza 1927, 548-552.

FANTOZZI A., *La riforma osservante dei monasteri delle clarisse nell'Italia centrale*, in *Archivum Franciscanum Historicum*, 23 (1930).

KERN L., *A propos du mouvement des flagellants de 1260. S. Bevignate de Pérouse*, in *Festschrift Gustav Schnurer*. Paderborn 1930.

PACETTI D., *La predicazione di S. Bernardino da Siena a Perugia e ad Assisi nel 1425*, in Collectanea Franciscana, 9 (1939).

FANTOZZI A. - BUGHETTI B., *Il Terz'Ordine Francescano in Perugia dal sec. XIII al sec. XIX*, in *Archivum Franciscanum Historicum*, 33 (1940).

PANTONI A., *Santa Caterina di Perugia. La storia*, in *Benedictina*, 5 (1951).

IDEM, *Santa Caterina di Perugia. I documenti*, Ibid., 6 (1952).

ASTUTI M. - MELIS F., *L'esplorazione dei fondi storico-economici dell'Archivio di S. Pietro di Perugia*, Ibid.

PANTONI A., *Monasteri sotto la regola benedettina a Perugia e dintorni*, Ibid., 8 (1954).

TABARELLI C., *Il monastero di S. Pietro di Perugia e la Repubblica del Trasimeno (1797-1799) nel racconto del Bini*, Ibid.

LECCISSOTTI T. - TABARELLI C., *Le carte dell'Archivio di San Pietro di Perugia*, Milano 1956.

PANTONI A., *Chiese perugine dipendenti da monasteri. Note storiche e topografiche*, in *Benedictina*, 11 (1957).

AA.VV., *Il movimento dei Disciplinati nel Settimo Centenario dal suo inizio*, Perugia 1962.

KAEPPELI T., *Inventari di libri di San Domenico di Perugia (1430-80)*, Roma 1962.

MAJARELLI S. - NICOLINI U., *Il Monte dei poveri di Perugia. Periodo delle origini (1462-1474)*, Perugia 1962.

NICOLINI U., *La vita del clero a Perugia nei secoli XI e XII*, in *La vita comune del clero nei secoli XI e XII*, 2, Milano 1962.

PIZZONI C., *La confraternita dell'Annunziata in Perugia*, in *Il movimento dei Disciplinati nel Settimo Centenario dal suo inizio*, Perugia 1962.

NICOLINI U., *Nuove testimonianze su fra Raniero Fasani e i suoi Disciplinati*, in BDSPU, 60 (1963).

BONMANN O., *Problemi critici riguardo ai cosiddetti «Statuta Bernardiniana» di Perugia (1421-1426)*, in *Studi Francescani*, 62 (1965).

MONTANARI M., *Mille anni della chiesa di S. Pietro e del suo patrimonio*, Foligno 1966.

NICOLINI U., *Ricerche sulla sede di fra Raniero Fasani fuori di porta Sole a Perugia*, in BDSPU, 63 (1966).

BALEONUS ASTUR, *Colomba da Rieti*, Roma 1967.

Convegno storico per il millennio dell'Abbazia di S. Pietro in Perugia, in BDSPU, 64 (1967).

TABARELLI C., *Liber contractuum (1331-32) dell'Abbazia Benedettina di San Pietro in Perugia*, Perugia 1967.

GROHMANN A., *In margine ad una carta geografica delle chiese, dei monasteri e degli ospedali della diocesi e del contado di Perugia nel sec. XIV*, in *Annali della Facoltà di Scienze Politiche dell'Università di Perugia*, 1970-72, 11 n.s., 1.

GABRIJELCIC A., *Alle origini del Seminario di Perugia (1559-1600)*, in BDSPU, 68 (1971).

NICOLINI U., *I Minori Osservanti di Monteripido e lo «Scriptorium» delle clarisse di Monteluce in Perugia nei secoli XV e XVI*, in *Picenum Seraphicum*, 8 (1971).

AA.VV., *Risultati e prospettive della ri-*

cerca sul movimento dei Disciplinati, Perugia 1972.

VALERI E., La fraternita dell'Ospedale di S. Maria della Misericordia in Perugia nei secoli XIII-XVII, Perugia 1972.

BICO G.M., La confraternita di S. Antonio Abate in Perugia, in Annali della Facoltà di Lettere e Filosofia dell'Università di Perugia, Perugia 1973.

PECUGI FOP M., La biblioteca di Monteripido: manoscritti e incunaboli, Santa Maria degli Angeli 1976.

CASAGRANDE G., Documenti inediti sui Frati della Penitenza a Perugia nei secoli XIII e XIV, in Studi Francescani, 74 (1977).

IDEM, Penitenti e Disciplinati a Perugia e loro rapporti con gli Ordini Mendicanti, in Mélanges de l'École française de Rome, 89 (1977).

LUNGAROTTI POLLIDORI M.C., Documenti pontifici del monastero di S. Pietro di Perugia (sec. XV), in Benedictina, 24 (1977).

LUNGAROTTI M.C. - TITTARELLI L., Descrizione della città e della diocesi di Perugia. Un manoscritto del XVI secolo, in Annali della Facoltà di Scienze Politiche dell'Università di Perugia (1973-76), 13 n.s., Perugia 1977.

RONCETTI M., La chiesa e il monastero olivetano di S. Secondo nell'Isola Polvese, in BDSPU, 74 (1977).

TABARELLI C., Documentazione notarile perugina sul convento di Monteripido nei secoli XIV e XV, Perugia 1977.

CASAGRANDE G., Il monastero di S. Agnese in Perugia nei secoli XIV e XV, in Studi Francescani, 76 (1979).

GALLETTI A.I., Insediamento e primo sviluppo dei Frati Minori a Perugia, in Francescanesimo e società cittadina: l'esempio di Perugia, a cura di U. Nicolini, Perugia 1979.

Francescanesimo e società cittadina: l'esempio di Perugia, a cura di U. Nicolini, Perugia 1979.

CASAGRANDE G., Aspetti del Terz'Ordine Francescano a Perugia nella seconda metà del secolo XIV e nel XV, in Il movimento francescano della penitenza nella società medioevale, a cura di Mariano d'Alatri, Roma 1980.

CASAGRANDE G. - MONACCHIA P., Il monastero di Santa Giuliana a Perugia nel secolo XIII, in Benedictina, 27 (1980).

TOMMASI F., L'Ordine dei Templari a Perugia, in BDSPU, 78 (1981).

CASAGRANDE G., Gli iscritti della confraternita dei Disciplinati di San Francesco in Perugia, in Annali della Facoltà di Lettere e Filosofia dell'Università di Perugia, in corso di stampa.

IDEM, Pievi e parrocchie dipendenti dal Capitolo della Cattedrale di Perugia nel secolo XIII, Ibid., in corso di pubblicazione.

GALLETTI A.I., Sant'Ercolano, il grifo e le lasche. Note sull'immaginario collettivo nella città comunale, in Materiali di Storia, 4, in corso di stampa.

Il Memoriale di Monteluce, a cura di U. Nicolini, in corso di stampa.

ART

PASCOLI L., Vite dé pittori, scultori ed architetti perugini, Roma 1732.

MARIOTTI A., Lettera scritta al Sig. Ab. N.N. Romano per ragguagliarlo della chiesa di S. Ercolano di Perugia, Perugia 1775.

GALASSI F.M., Descrizione della chiesa di S. Lorenzo, Roma 1776.

MARIOTTI A., Lettere pittoriche perugine, Perugia 1788.

ORSINI B., Risposte alle lettere pittoriche del Signor Annibale Mariotti, Perugia 1791.

GALASSI F.M., Descrizione delle pitture di S. Pietro di Perugia, Perugia 1792.

ORSINI B., Dissertazione sull'antico tempio di S. Angiolo di Perugia, Perugia 1792.

ORSINI B., Memorie dei pittori perugini del sec. XVIII, Perugia 1806.

ANGELUCCI A., Della oreficeria perugina dal XIII alla prima metà del XVI secolo, Perugia 1853.

MARCHESI R., I lavori di architettura e pittura nella chiesa del Carmine in Perugia eseguiti da Vincenzo Baldini, Perugia 1856.

ROSSI-SCOTTI G.B., Il Palazzo del Popolo, Perugia 1864.

ROTELLI L., Il Duomo di Perugia, Perugia 1864.

ROSSI A., Saggio sugli svarioni seminati nell'opuscolo del Can. Luigi Rotelli sul Duomo di Perugia, Perugia 1864.

ROTELLI L., Risposta al Sig. Prof. Adamo Rossi autore del saggio di svarioni ecc..., Perugia 1864.

ROSSI A., Documenti inediti su fabbriche perugine del sec. XV, Perugia 1870.

ROSSI A., Gli orefici Roscetto, Perugia 1873.

ROSSI A., Maestri e lavori di legname in Perugia nei sec. XV e XVI, Perugia 1873.

ROSSI A., Storia artistica del Cambio di Perugia, Perugia 1874.

MANARI L., Cenno storico ed artistico della Basilica di S. Pietro in Perugia. Documenti e note di cenni storico-artistici della Basilica di S. Pietro in Perugia, in L'Apologetico, 1864-66.

CERNICCHI G., The Cathedral of Perugia, Perugia 1884.

LUPATTELLI A., Catalogo dei quadri che si conservano nella Pinacoteca Vannucci di Perugia, Perugia 1885.

ROSSI A., La Piazza del Sopramuro in Perugia, Perugia 1887.

LUPATTELLI A., Storia della pittura in Perugia, Foligno 1895.

LUPATTELLI A., Delle immagini della Madonna delle Grazie in Perugia, Foligno 1898.

BELLUCCI A., Sulla scala esterna del Palazzo del Popolo, Perugia 1899.

MONTESPERELLI Z., Brevi cenni storici sulla Accademia di Belle Arti di Perugia, Perugia 1899.

DEGLI AZZI G., Il Collegio della Mercanzia, Perugia 1901.

DEGLI AZZI G., Notizie storico-artistiche tratte dall'archivio del Collegio del Cambio, Perugia 1902.

LUPATTELLI A., Dell'importanza religiosa, storica ed artistica dell'ex chiesa di S. Francesco al Prato di Perugia, Roma 1902.

RICCI E., L'immagine di Maria SS. delle Grazie nel Duomo di Perugia, Perugia 1902.

GRAHRAM J.C., The problem of Fiorenzo di Lorenzo, Perugia 1903.

LUPATTELLI A., Benedetto XI in Perugia. Suo monumento sepolcrale, sue reliquie, Perugia 1903.

BOMBE W., Benedetto Bonfigli, Berlin 1904.

MANZONI L., Statuti e matricole dell'arte dei pittori delle città di Firenze, Perugia e Siena, Roma 1904.

WEBER S., Fiorenzo di Lorenzo, Strassburg 1904.

VENTURI A., La fonte di piazza in Perugia, in L'Arte 1905.

BOMBE W., Gonfaloni umbri, Perugia 1907.

LUPATTELLI A., Mostra di antica arte umbra in Perugia, Roma 1907.

Mostra d'antica arte umbra, Catalogo, Perugia 1907.

GNOLI U., L'arte umbra alla mostra di Perugia, Bergamo 1908.

LUPATTELLI A., La Pinacoteca Vannucci in Perugia, Perugia 1909.

RICCI E., La prima Chiesa dedicata a S. Elisabetta d'Ungheria, S. Maria degli Angeli 1909.

BOMBE W., L'acquedotto e la fontana di Perugia, in Arte e Storia, 1910.

VIVIANI D., Il Tempio di S. Angelo in Perugia, Perugia 1911.

BOMBE W., Geschichte der peruginer Malerei bis zu Perugino und Pinturicchio, Berlin 1912.

BOMBE W., Les tissus et les dentelles de Pérouse, in L'art decoratif, 1912.

TARCHI U., Sul ripristino e restauro del Palazzo del Capitano del Popolo in Perugia, Perugia 1917.

AA.VV., Chiesa e Convento di S. Maria Nuova, in Arte e Storia, 1919.

CECCHINI G., Saggio sulla cultura artistica e letteraria in Perugia nel sec. XIX, Foligno 1921.

SALMI M., Gli affreschi ricordati dal Vasari in S. Domenico a Perugia, in Bollettino d'Arte, 1921-22.

MUNOZ A., Matteo Gattaponi da Gubbio e il chiostro di S. Giuliana in Perugia, in Bollettino d'Arte, 1922-23.

GNOLI U., I documenti su Pietro Perugino, Perugia 1923.

GNOLI U., Pietro Perugino, Spoleto 1923.

GNOLI U., Pittori e miniatori nell'Umbria, Spoleto 1923.

ANSIDEI V., La chiesa di S. Francesco al Prato in Perugia, Città di Castello 1925.

URBINI G., Arte umbra, Città di Castello 1925.

GNOLI U., La Pinacoteca di Perugia, Firenze 1927.

BOMBE W., Urkunden zur geschichte der peruginer Malerei im 16 Jahrhundert, Leipzig 1929.

RICCI E., La chiesa di S. Prospero e i pittori del Duecento in Perugia, Perugia 1929.

CANUTI F., Il Perugino, Siena 1931.

CECCHINI G., La galleria Nazionale dell'Umbria, Roma 1932.

ROCCHI M., Le tovaglie perugine, in Rassegna marchigiana, 1932.

SANTAGATA G., La chiesa del Gesù di Perugia, Perugia 1934.

TARCHI U., L'arte nell'Umbria e nella Sabina, voll. 1-4, Milano 1936-1940; Appendice, 1954.

S.A., Notizie intorno alla chiesa parrocchiale di S. Stefano a Perugia, Perugia 1938.

MARIANI V., Una sconosciuta scultura di Arnolfo di Cambio, in Rivista del R. Istituto d'Archeologia e Storia dell'Arte, 1938.

BOCCOLINI G., Caratteri degli influssi toscani nell'architettura umbra del Quattrocento e Francesco di Guido da Settignano, in Atti del II Convegno Nazionale di Storia dell'Architettura, Assisi 1937, Roma 1939.

MARIANI V., Gli assetati di Arnolfo di Cambio, Roma 1939.

GURRIERI O., Il tempio di S. Angelo in Perugia, Perugia 1946.

GAMBA C., Pittura umbra del Rinascimento, Novara 1949.

CELLINI P., Della fontana di Perugia, in Paragone, 1951.

GURRIERI O., Il Palazzo dell'Università Italiana per Stranieri, in Perusia, 1951.

NICCO-FASOLA G., La fontana di Arnolfo, in Commentari, 1951.

NICCO-FASOLA G., La fontana di Perugia, Roma 1951.

SANTI F., Mostra della pittura dell'800 a Perugia, Catalogo, Perugia 1951.

GUARDABASSI M. - SANTI F., Il portale maggiore del Palazzo dei Priori in Perugia, Perugia 1953.

CECCHINI G., L'Accademia di Belle Arti di Perugia, Perugia s.d. (ma 1954).

MARTELLI G., Il nuovo ordinamento della Galleria Nazionale dell'Umbria, in

Bollettino d'Arte, 1955.

Santi F., *La Galleria Nazionale dell'Umbria in Perugia*, Roma 1955.

Santi F., *Ritrovamento di oreficerie medioevali in S. Domenico di Perugia*, in *Bollettino d'Arte*, 1955.

Venturi A., *Il Perugino. Gli affreschi del Cambio*, (a cura di G. Carandente), Roma 1955.

Sessant'anni di vita perugina nelle vecchie fotografie (1855-1915), Catalogo della mostra, Perugia 1956.

Bianchi L., *La fontana di Perugia e il suo architetto*, in *Atti del V Convegno Nazionale di Storia dell'Architettura*, Perugia 1948, Firenze 1957.

Boccassini G., *Le tele dell'Aliense a Perugia*, in *Arte Veneta*, 1957.

Gurrieri O., *La chiesa di S. Agostino di Perugia e le sue vicende architettoniche*, in *Atti del V Convegno Nazionale di Storia dell'Architettura*, Perugia 1948, Firenze 1957.

Labò M., *Galeazzo Alessi a Genova*, in *Atti del V Convegno Nazionale di Storia dell'Architettura*, Perugia 1948, Firenze 1957.

Pickert L.C., *Gli artisti tedeschi a Perugia nel sec. XIX*, Perugia 1957.

Camesasca E., *Tutta la pittura del Perugino*, Milano 1959.

Carli E., *Il Pintoricchio*, Milano 1960.

Cellini P., *Giuochi d'acqua a Perugia*, in *Paragone*, 1960.

Duranti I., *La «Giuditta» del Sassoferrato dell'Abbazia di San Pietro in Perugia ed il suo disegno*, in BDSPU, 57 (1960).

Santi F., *Appunti per la storia urbanistica di Perugia*, in *Urbanistica*, 1960.

Santi F., *Considerazioni sulla fontana di Arnolfo a Perugia*, in *Commentari*, 1960.

Santi F., *L'altare di Agostino di Duccio in S. Domenico di Perugia*, in *Bollettino d'Arte*, 1960.

Gualdi F., *Contributi a Berto di Giovanni pittore perugino*, in *Commentari*, 1961.

Montanari M., *È di Bernardo Rossellino il progetto del campanile di San Pietro in Perugia*, in BDSPU, 58 (1961).

Santi F., *Gli affreschi di Lazzaro Vasari in S. Maria Nuova di Perugia*, in *Bollettino d'Arte*, 1961.

Crosara A., *Il messaggio figurato della Fonte Maggiore con un cenno alla simbologia di altri monumenti di Perugia*, in BDSPU, 59 (1962).

Santi F., *La nicchia di S. Bernardino a Perugia*, Milano 1963.

Bovini G., *Sarcofagi tardo-antichi dell'Umbria con figurazioni cristiane*, in *Atti del II Convegno di Studi Umbri*, Perugia 1965.

De Angelis d'Ossat G., *Classicismo e problematica nelle architetture paleocristiane dell'Umbria*, Ibid.

Salmi M., *Tardo antico e Alto Medioevo in Umbria*, Ibid.

De Angelis d'Ossat G., *La chiesa di S. Angelo di Perugia*, in *Corsi di cultura sull'arte ravennate e bizantina*, 1966.

Mostra documentaria e iconografica dell'abbazia benedettina di S. Pietro in Perugia, Catalogo, Perugia 1966.

Raspi Serra J., *La scultura dell'Umbria centro-meridionale dall'VIII al IX secolo*, in *Atti del III Convegno di Studi Umbri*, Perugia 1966.

Nessi S., *Documenti sull'arte umbra. I. I pittori perugini del secolo XIII*, in *Commentari*, 1967.

Zanoli A., *Perugia. S. Bernardino*, in *Tesori d'arte cristiana*, Bologna 1967.

Hoffmann-Curtius K., *Das Programm der Fontana Maggiore in Perugia*, Düsseldorf 1968.

Santi F., *Un altro «scriba» di Arnolfo per la fontana perugina del 1281*, in *Paragone*, 1968.

Caleca A., *Miniature in Umbria. La Biblioteca Capitolare di Perugia*, Pisa 1969.

Romanini A.M., *Arnolfo di Cambio*, Milano 1969.

Camesasca E., *L'opera completa del Perugino*, Milano 1969.

Martinelli V., *Una testa sconosciuta di Giovanni Pisano a Perugia (e il problema di Giovanni architetto)*, in *Momenti del marmo. Scritti per duecento anni dell'Accademia di Carrara*, Roma 1969.

Ricci E., *La chiesa dell'Immacolata Concezione e di San Filippo Neri (Chiesa Nuova) in Perugia*, Perugia 1969.

Santi F., *La Galleria Nazionale dell'Umbria*, Roma 1969.

Martini A., *Il Palazzo dei Priori a Perugia*, in *Palladio*, 1970.

Santi F., *L'affresco baglionesco della Galleria Nazionale dell'Umbria*, in *Commentari*, 1970.

Ballo G., *Dottori aereopittore futurista*, Roma 1970.

Martinelli V., *Arnolfo a Perugia*, in *Atti del VI Convegno di Studi Umbri*, Perugia 1971.

Pickert L.C., *Disegni umbri di artisti tedeschi dell'800* (con nota introduttiva di P. Scarpellini), Perugia 1971.

Santi F., *Di una scomparsa fontana duecentesca a Cortona e dei suoi rapporti con la Fontana Maggiore di Perugia*, in *Atti del VI Convegno di Studi Umbri*, Perugia 1971.

Scarpellini P. - Nicolini U., *La Biblioteca Capitolare di Perugia*, in BDSPU, 68 (1971).

Cutini Zazzerini C., *Sulla datazione del grifo perugino*, in BDSPU, 69 (1972).

Pardi R., *Ricerche di architettura religiosa medioevale in Umbria*, Perugia 1972.

Santi F., *Nota sul Palazzo dei Priori a Perugia*, in BDSPU, 69 (1972).

Boskovits M., *Pittura umbra e marchigiana fra Medioevo e Rinascimento*, Firenze 1973.

Cantelli G., *Il mobile umbro*, Milano 1973.

Longhi R., *La pittura umbra della prima metà del Trecento*, Firenze 1973.

Martini A., *Critica e storiografia del Palazzo dei Priori*, in *Annali della Facoltà di Lettere e Filosofia dell'Università di Perugia*, 1973.

Algeri G., *Alessi in Umbria* in *Galeazzo Alessi e l'architettura del Cinquecento. Atti del Convegno Internazionale di studi*, Genova 1974.

Ascani Maddoli C., *Appunti e note su alcune opere di G. Alessi in Umbria*, Ibid.

Biavati G., *Precisazioni su Giovanni Andrea Carlone*, in *Paragone*, 1974.

Scarpellini P. - Mancini F.F., *Le raccolte d'arte dell'Accademia di Perugia*, 1974.

Catalogo del Museo dell'Università degli Studi di Perugia «G.B. Vermiglioli», Perugia 1975.

Emiliani A., *Federico Barocci*, Catalogo della mostra, Bologna 1975.

Mengarelli A., *Origini e sviluppo dell'Oratorio perugino di S. Filippo Neri*, Perugia 1975.

Pardi R., *Monumenti medioevali umbri*, Perugia 1975.

Scalpellini P., *Il pittore perugino Mariano d'Antonio ed il Palazzo dei Priori nel Quattrocento*, in *Annali della Facoltà di Lettere e Filosofia dell'Università di Perugia*, Perugia 1975.

Casale V. - Falcidia G. - Toscano B., *Pittura del '600 e '700. Ricerche in Umbria 1*, Treviso 1976.

Santi F., *Gonfaloni umbri del Rinascimento*, Perugia 1976.

Santi F., *La facciata originale dell'ales-*

siana chiesa di S. Maria del Popolo a Perugia, in BDSPU, 73 (1976).

AA.VV., *San Francesco al Prato: dall'abbandono al ripristino*, Perugia 1977.

Bellosi L., *La sala dei Notari, Marino da Perugia e un ante quem per il problema di Assisi*, in *Per Maria Cionini Visani*, Torino 1977.

Cresti M.V. - Mancini F.F. - Sapori G., *Cento disegni dell'Accademia di Belle Arti di Perugia. XVII-XIX secolo*, Catalogo della mostra, Roma 1977.

Mostra dei disegni dei monumenti perugini ed umbri dall'era etrusca al secolo XVIII dell'architetto Ugo Tarchi, Catalogo, Perugia 1977.

Scarpellini P., *Le fonti critiche relative ai pittori umbri del Rinascimento*, in *Atti del IX Convegno di Studi Umbri*, Perugia 1977.

Bistoni M.G. - Casagrande G. - Monacchia P., *Bino Sozi architetto della Maestà delle Volte a Perugia*, in *Esercizi*, 1978.

Mancini F.F., *Figure e paesi di Pietro Montanini*, Ibid.

Scarpellini P., *Per la pittura perugina del Trecento. I. Il Maestro di Paciano*, Ibid.

Strehlke C.B., *A bronze Lion and Panther in the Wadsworth Atheneum Hartford*, Ibid.

AA.VV., *Guida all'arte contemporanea in Umbria*, Perugia 1979.

Mancini F.F., *Identificazione di Pietro di Galeotto*, in *Esercizi*, 1979.

Perari M.E., *Anton Maria e Domenico Garbi*, Ibid.

Sapori G., *Per un riesame di Giannicola di Paolo*, Ibid.

Scarpellini P., *Osservazioni su una Crocifissione miniata nell'antifonario 2798 della Biblioteca Augusta di Perugia*, in *Atti del I Convegno di Storia della Miniatura*, Firenze 1979.

Barroero L. - Falcidia G. - Pansecchi F. -Toscano B., *Pittura del '600 e '700. Ricerche in Umbria 2*, Treviso 1980.

Cutini Zazzerini C., *Nuovi documenti del 1278 sulla Fontana Maggiore*, Perugia 1980.

Sapori G., *Notizie su Giovan Battista Lombardelli*, in *Storia dell'Arte*, 1980.

Scarpellini P., *Per la pittura perugina del Trecento. II. Il Maestro del 1320 ed il Maestro ironico*, in *Esercizi*, 1980.

Tiberia V., *L'Oratorio di S. Agostino a Perugia. Appunti per una storia dal XVI al XIX secolo*, in *Storia dell'Arte*, 1980. *Gli affreschi di Paolo III a Castel Sant'Angelo. 1543-1548*, Catalogo della mostra, Roma 1981.

Marabottini A., *Alcune considerazioni sulla pala di S. Maria del Popolo a Perugia*, in *Esercizi*, 1981.

Boskovits M., *Gli affreschi della Sala dei Notari a Perugia e la pittura in Umbria alla fine del XIII secolo*, in *Bollettino d'Arte*, 1981.

Riess J.B., *Uno studio iconografico della decorazione ed affresco del 1297 nella Sala dei Notari a Perugia*, in *Bollettino d'Arte*, 1981.

Scarpellini P., *Per la pittura perugina del Trecento. III. Il Maestro di Monte del Lago*, in *Esercizi*, 1981.

Casale V., *Come distinguere e considerare Benedetto Bandiera e Simeone Ciburri*, in *Atti del XII Convegno di Studi Umbri*, Spoleto 1982.

Mancini F.F., *Profilo di Giovanni Antonio Scaramuccia*, Ibid.

Mariotti-Puerini A., *Aspetti iconografici della decorazione di S. Pietro a Perugia*, Ibid.

Santi F., *Precisazioni su Vincenzo Danti*, Ibid.

Scarpellini P., *Giovan Battista Caporali e la cultura artistica perugina nella pri-*

ma metà del Cinquecento, Ibid.

TEODORI B., *Aspetti del baroccismo perugino: Benedetto Bandiera, Felice e Vincenzo Pellegrini*, Ibid.

GURRIERI O., *I tesori artistici di Perugia in Italia e nel mondo*, Perugia s.d.

ARCHEOLOGY

VERMIGLIOLI G.B., *Antiche iscrizioni perugine*, Perugia, 1 (1833), 2 (1834).

IDEM, *Il sepolcro dei Volumni scoperto in Perugia*, Perugia 1840.

CONESTABILE G., *Dei monumenti di Perugia etrusca e romana, della letteratura e bibliografia perugina*, 1-3, Perugia 1855-56; 4, Perugia 1870.

LUPATTELLI A., *Indicazione degli oggetti più importanti che si trovano nei Musei di Antichità Etrusca, Romana e Medioevale esistenti nell'Università di Perugia*, Perugia 1882.

DENNIS G., *The Cities and Cemeteries of Etruria*, 2 London 1883.

BELLUCCI G., *Guida alle collezioni del museo etrusco-romano in Perugia*, Perugia 1910.

ZALAPY E., *La tomba etrusca dei Velimni*, in BDSPU, 24 (1920).

GALLI E., *Il museo funerario del Palazzone all'Ipogeo dei Volumni*, Firenze 1921.

PAOLETTI A., *Studi su Perugia etrusca. Necropoli del Frontone, di Monteluce e dello Sperandio*, Perugia 1923.

BUONAMICI G., *L'Ipogeo e l'iscrizione etrusca di S. Manno presso Perugia*, in *Studi Etruschi*, 2 (1928).

BANTI L., *Contributo alla storia e alla topografia del territorio perugino*, in *Studi Etruschi*, 10 (1936).

CAMPELLI V., *La cinta murale di Perugia*, in *Rivista dell'Ist. Naz. d'Archeologia e Storia dell'Arte*, 5 (1936).

RIIS P.J., *Etruscan City Gates in Perugia*, in *Acta Archaelogica*, 5 (1939).

SHAW CH., *Etruscan Perugia*, Baltimora 1939.

VON GERKEN A. - NESSER SCHMIDT F., *Das Grab der Volumnier bei Perugia*, in *Römische Mitteilungen*, 1942.

PIEROTTI A. - CALZONI M., *Ricerche su Perugia etrusca*, in *Studi Etruschi*, 21 (1950-51).

GIGLIOLI G.Q., *Il sarcofago dello Sperandio del Museo Archeologico di Perugia*, in *Archeologia Classica*, 4 (1952).

LUGLI G., *La tecnica edilizia romana*, Roma 1957.

JOHNSTONE A.M., *The Etruscan Life in Perugia*, Firenze 1964.

CALZONI U., *Museo Archeologico Nazionale dell'Umbria. Perugia. Sezione preistorica*, 3ª ed., Roma 1971.

DAREGGI G., *Urne del territorio perugino. Quaderni dell'Istituto di Archeologia dell'Università di Perugia*, 1, Roma 1972.

BOITANI F. - CATALDI M. - PASQUINUCCI M., *Le città etrusche*, Verona 1973.

STOPPONI S., *Il pozzo Sorbello di Perugia*, in *Quaderni dell'Istituto di Archeologia dell'Università di Perugia*, 2, Roma 1973.

MATTEINI CHIARI M., *La tomba del Faggeto in territorio perugino*, in *Quaderni dell'Istituto di Archeologia dell'Università di Perugia*, 3, Roma 1975.

FERUGLIO A.E., *Complessi tombali con urne nel territorio di Perugia*, in *Atti dell'incontro sui caratteri dell'ellenismo nelle urne etrusche*, Firenze 1977.

CENCIAIOLI L., *I capitelli romani a Perugia*, in *Annali della Facoltà di Lettere e Filosofia dell'Università di Perugia*, 15 (1977-78), n.s. 1.

MATTEINI CHIARI M., *Porte minori della cinta perugina: le postierle della Cupa e della Conca*, in *Nuovi Quaderni dell'Istituto di Archeologia dell'Università di Perugia*, 1 (1979).

DE ALBENTIIS E., *Il mosaico del Museo Archeologico di Perugia*, in *Annali della Facoltà di Lettere e Filosofia dell'Università di Perugia*, 16 (1979-80), 3.

DEFOSSE P., *Les remparts de Pérouse. Contribution à l'histoire de l'urbanisme préromaine*, in *Mélanges de l'École française de Rome*, 92 (1980).

GAGGIOTTI M. - MANCONI D. - MERCANDO L. - VERZAR M., *Umbria-Marche*, Bari 1980.

BIBLIOGRAPHIES AND INVENTORIES

VERMIGLIOLI G.B., *Bibliografia storico-perugina*, Perugia 1823.

IDEM, *Biografie degli scrittori perugini*, Perugia 1828-29.

BELLUCCI A., *Inventario dei manoscritti della Biblioteca Comunale di Perugia*, in *Inventario dei manoscritti delle Biblioteche d'Italia*, Forlì 1895.

IDEM, *Inventario dei manoscritti della Biblioteca Dominicini di Perugia*, Forlì 1892.

CECCHINI G., *L'archivio storico del comune di Perugia*, Roma 1956.

Indici del Bollettino della Deputazione di Storia Patria per l'Umbria, 1 (1895) - 51 (1954), a cura di O. Marinelli, Perugia 1957.

MARINELLI O., *Le confraternite di Perugia dalle origini al sec. XIX*, Perugia 1965.

MINCIOTTI C., *Le carte del fondo Danzetta dell'Archivio di Stato di Perugia*, in *Rassegna storica del Risorgimento*, 60 (1973).

CASAGRANDE G., *Inventario dell'Archivio del monastero della Beata Colomba*, in BDSPU, 73 (1976).

Indici del Bollettino della Deputazione di Storia Patria per l'Umbria, 54 (1957) - 75 (1978), a cura di M.L. Cianini Pierotti, Perugia 1980.

LETI G. - TITTARELLI L., *Le fonti per lo studio della popolazione della diocesi di Perugia dalla metà del XVI secolo al 1860*, 1, Gubbio 1976; 2, ivi 1978; 3, Perugia 1980.

HISTORICAL AND ARTISTICS PERIODICALS

Giornale di Erudizione Artistica, Voll. 6, Perugia 1872-1877.

Augusta Perusia 1906-1908; n.s. 1955-1956.

Rassegna d'Arte Umbra 1910-1921.

Perusia 1929-1937; n.s. 1949-1954.

MUSIC AND THEATRE

ROSSI SCOTTI G.B., *Della vita e delle opere di Francesco Morlacchi*, Perugia 1861.

RICCI E., *Organi ed organisti perugini*, Perugia 1910.

GUARDABASSI F., *Appunti storici sull'Accademia civica del teatro Morlacchi di Perugia*, Perugia 1927.

PASCUCCI G., *La nobile Accademia del Pavone e il suo teatro*, Perugia 1927.

GURRIERI O., *Il teatro Turreno in Perugia dal 1879 al 1954*, in *Augusta Perusia*, 16 (1955).

SABATINI R., *Medaglioni musicali umbri*, Perugia 1968.

ATLAS W.A., *The Accademia degli Unisoni: a Music Academy Renaissance Perugia*, in *A Musical Offering: Essays in Honor of M. Bernstein*, New York 1977.

BRUMANA B., *Luigi Caruso e la cappella musicale del Duomo di Perugia dal 1788 al 1823*, in *Nuova Rivista Musicale Italiana*, 1977. -

SABATINI R., *Francesco Morlacchi (1784-1841)*, Perugia 1977.

BRUMANA B., *Per una storia dell'oratorio musicale a Perugia nei secoli XVII e XVIII*, in *Esercizi*, 3 (1980).

PASCALE M., *Vincenzo Cossa e l'ambiente musicale perugino tra Cinquecento e Seicento*, in *Atti del XII Convegno di Studi Umbri*, Spoleto 1982.

NAME INDEX

PLACE INDEX

INDEX

Printed in
at the lithographic workshop of
LA FOTOMETALGRAFICA EMILIANA
San Lazzaro di Savena - Bologna